American Regional Rooms

American Regional Rooms

A NEW PERSPECTIVE ON TRADITIONAL DESIGN

MICHAEL HENRY ADAMS

MALLARD PRESS

An Imprint of BDD Promotional Book Company, Inc.
666 Fifth Avenue
New York, N.Y. 10103

A FRIEDMAN GROUP BOOK
Published by MALLARD PRESS
An Imprint of BDD Promotional Book Company, Inc.
666 Fifth Avenue
New York, N.Y. 10103

Mallard Press and its accompanying design and logo are trademarks of
BDD Promotional Book Company, Inc.

ISBN 0-7924-5541-X

AMERICAN REGIONAL ROOMS
A New Perspective on Traditional Design
was prepared and produced by
Michael Friedman Publishing Group, Inc.
15 West 26th Street
New York, New York 10010

Editor: Sharyn Rosart
Art Director: Jeff Batzli
Designer: Susan Livingston
Photography Editor: Daniella Jo Nilva

Typeset by The Typecrafters, Inc.
Color separations by Excel Graphic Arts Co.
Printed and bound in Hong Kong by Leefung-Asco Printers Ltd.

Dedication

For my beloved grandmother Louise Blanks who first encouraged appreciation of beauty, and great friends Suzanne Slesin, Markiver Grisom, and Jeannette Dempsey.

⸺⊱⊰⊱⊰⸺

Acknowledgments

American Regional Rooms was realized with the generous assistance of countless people across the country who contributed examples of regional styles, offered advice, shared research, and opened their homes. A partial list of those to whom I shall ever be indebted include my dear friend Suzanne Slesin, my invaluable editor Sharyn Rosart (who transformed scribbling into a readable narrative), designer Sue Livingston, photo editor Daniella Jo Nilva, historians John Franklin Miller, Robin Middelton, Carolyn Kent, and J. S. Ellenberger, and photographer Alex McLean. Thanks also to Mario Buatta, Chippy Irvine, Thomas Britt, Shirley Driks, Stanley Barrows, Kevin Wolfe, John Reddick, George Goodwill, Lanna Turner, Curtis Q. Phelps, Steven Brody, Max Frescoln, Harold and Martha Dolly, Hal Bromm, Doneley Meris, Dr. Brenda Bennett, Ronald Melichar, Dr. Richard Dudley, Ronald Wagner, James Phalau, Laura and Bush Jones, and Patricia Juviler.

CONTENTS

© Alex McLean

INTRODUCTION

10

PRECEDING PAGE: *At a gray shingled house by the sea, simple elements – 1920s wicker furniture, a rag rug, and an old grained chest used as a coffee table – create all-American charm.*

ABOVE: *A dish of coral branches, a silver cat, and a paper fan enliven a formal Mid-Atlantic room.*

Today more than ever, there is a growing admiration for the distinctive charm of America's regional rooms. Settled by people who came from all over the world to seek a better way of life, the United States has a proud tradition of diversity. This has made America a marvelous mosaic of cultures. No matter where in this country they settled, our ancestors brought to the new world something of the old country – from the way they talked to the meals they made. Their traditions were exemplified in

material culture as well – particularly in choices of architecture and home decoration. In each state, region, or sometimes even in adjoining communities, different cultural traditions were revealed in the styles of houses and their interiors. Yet the old customs were not entirely traditional because by adapting the homes they had known before to a new environment with changed conditions and possibilities these new Americans created a new, richly varied aesthetic. They also created the American regional room.

No less than local food favorites, such as delectable buckwheat cakes with butter and golden maple syrup or fiery Texas chili con carne, regional rooms remind us of our roots. Like regional cuisine, they represent a marriage of the old world, tried and true, and the best qualities of the new world. The results range from the brightly painted, paneled parlors of gray-shingled New England dwellings to the low, cool tile- or brick-floored rooms found in adobe ranches from Texas to California.

These, of course, are but two of a host of popular American regional room types. During the trip across the ocean and continent, the original styles on which these rooms were based evolved to suit their new environments. Generally, a good deal of unnecessary decoration and clutter was eliminated, and much in the way of practicality, comfort, and

Whimsical treasures like the antique French bottle and a magnifying glass with a carved ivory rose handle pictured below are reminiscent of pleasant trips and beloved relations and friends.

convenience was added. These transitional refinements formed uniquely American styles with a decorative panache second to none.

In the past, American regional rooms were implicitly linked to regional architecture. The recently expanding popularity of regional rooms has been at least in part because of the movement to preserve old buildings. Much of the pleasure of visiting such unique American cities as Charleston, Albuquerque, Boston, St. Louis, Carmel, or Cincinnati has come from knowing that the customs, accent, style, scenery, and rooms of one region are likely to be excitingly different from those where you come from. In recent years, however, many of the regional differences have faded. The simple joys of discovery in traveling across the country have begun to disappear. Thanks to television, movies, and magazines promoting conformity, the trend in America has been increasingly toward homogeneity and sameness. Identical shopping malls, fast-food strips, and anonymous buildings are found all over the country.

The good news, though, is that many people are starting to react to the loss of distinctiveness. After generations of consciously rejecting their ethnic or cultural identities in an attempt to assimilate, Americans are once again taking pride in their heritage and expressing it in their homes. The

© Alex McLean

Oil paintings by the early twentieth-century Romanian artist Eustache Stoenesco and bright splashes of turquoise are points of focus in this all-white room.

12

American regional room has been an important manifestation of this reawakening.

A friend recently told me a story that shows how profoundly certain keepsakes can connect us to those who came before us. "Inheriting my grandmother's quilt was like getting a Rembrandt," she said. "It had always been around, taken for granted. When I was younger I didn't realize how important or valuable it was. It kept me warm when I'd stay over, but—well it's awful to say—I was ashamed of it. I really longed for Grandma to get a modern electric blanket like the pink one my best friend's grandmother had. I didn't know then that grandma's slightly worn patchwork quilt was made from pieces of dresses she and her sisters had worn or that it had taken four women in our family a week's worth of spare time to make or that it was on the bed when my mom was born. I only use it as a bedspread now so I'll be able to pass it on."

Many people have lost such family treasures as quilts, china, or old rocking chairs—items that can bring a room to life. Yet even if you're fortunate enough to have Aunt May's fine old mahogany furniture, it's not always so easy to determine how to fit it into your smallish contemporary condo.

American Regional Rooms is meant as a guide to assist you with this and other aspects of regional American decorating. Today, most families are composites of cultural backgrounds. Whether you're trying to reconcile inherited antiques from each side of the family or your spouse's collection of blue and white Staffordshire china with your assemblage of trompe l'oeil painted tin boxes, the business of devising a harmonious decor can be confusing. Combined with the overwhelming number of choices available in showrooms and catalogs, decorating in a regional style might seem an impossibility. However, it is possible to have an eventful homescape that reflects the taste and heritage of the entire clan without chaos. Furthermore, exposed as we are nowadays to the cultural and artistic wealth of the entire world, there's no excuse anymore for settling for one safe style in a beige room.

American Regional Rooms offers the perfect antidote to a bland beige environment, with descriptions of and suggestions for decorating in a wide variety of regional styles. Interior design of the South differs from that of the Southwest, just as the look of Los Angeles is dissimilar from that of New York. Yet, finally, all of the wonderful regional

© Alex McLean

In the dining area of a great room, eighteenth-century Portuguese chairs, steer horns, and a modern steel framed table with a tiled top are all happily combined. The shuttered pass-through on the right wall enables either handy informal access to the kitchen or a convenient screen for unexpected disasters. A mirror used in an architectural way both expands the space visually and directs guests toward the hallway.

styles of decorating serve a common goal and need. They're all a means of expressing, in a tangible way, the meaning of "home, sweet home." This book is about helping you to capture in your own home, no matter how modest or modern, something of the flavor and atmosphere of your favorite regional room style. It is possible to achieve the American regional room without turning your house into either a showroom or a museum.

American Regional Rooms begins with a survey of outstanding examples of the main regional room types. You'll see rooms from "a-way down East," as they say in Maine, to "a-way out West"—with stops along the way to examine New England Traditional Mid-Atlantic Cutting-Edge, and Spanish Colonial rooms. Each type of decor is examined to reveal its distinguishing characteristics. Following the exploration of regional style, each chapter goes on to discuss how a designer might employ a regional format or even just introduce regional elements to evoke Charleston's ambience, the rustic charm of the Rocky Mountain lodge, or the modern flair of a New York loft.

Finally, *American Regional Rooms* provides basic specific suggestions to help you realize

regionally inspired spaces at home. There are tips on how to treat a vestibule or hallway as a mediating space that both separates and joins two rooms with different regional themes. There are even suggestions on how you might accomplish the once-taboo notion of combining elements from different regions in the same room. Unique and lovely rooms can be created in this fashion, so long as you are sensitive to the common origins of certain styles. For instance, both Italian and Spanish furniture pieces from the sixteenth to the eighteenth century look great in adobe houses. Because of its elemental simplicity, Shaker furniture can work wonderfully alongside a high-tech steel-framed chair or a chintz-covered Philadelphia wingback settee.

In addition to regional stylistic analysis, *American Regional Rooms* looks at uniquely American room innovations such as the all-American porch and the increasingly popular great room, which combines multiple functions in one envelope. Did you ever think that out of the garage or a spare upstairs bedroom you might be able to create a great room? With a sense of adventure, a little imagination, and *American Regional Rooms*, you can do this and much more.

THE NORTHEAST

PRECEDING PAGE: *A grouping of ladder-back chairs, polished brass candlesticks, and heirloom china, set against a backdrop of scrubbed floorboards and white-washed walls, makes an authentic Northeast room. The bay leaf garland and lilac bouquet are delightful touches that reflect the changing seasons.*

RIGHT: *An antique lantern provides an appropriate detail at a Nantucket doorway.*

16

As every American schoolchild knows, the Pilgrims landed at "New" Plymouth, on a big rock, in 1620. Although they found much in the Massachusetts Bay Colony to remind them of England, there were nevertheless a few surprises that took a little time to get used to. (No, I'm not referring to the *Mayflower*'s passengers' original intent to land in Virginia.) What was especially remarkable for the early New Englanders was that their new homeland was densely covered by primeval forest, abundant with game. Nothing like the incredible American woodlands had existed in Europe for centuries. Because wood was scarce in England, all but the elite, who built stately houses of brick and stone, built half-timbered dwellings. "Half-timbered" is an almost-literal expression. Although the heavy frameworks of these houses

were made from stout timbers of oak or elm, the walls consisted of woven basketwork made of branches, covered on the inside and outside with stucco or plaster or, in America, with clay. This was what English colonists were used to, so despite America's enormous forests, that's what they built in their new land—at least at first. Indeed, wherever the English settled along the Atlantic coast, they continued to look to England for stylistic inspiration and even for objects that weren't here.

The center of New England homes for the early settlers and even today is the chimney corner. Early on, the pioneers learned how to cut huge logs into long planks or clapboards, which were sawed in big pits. At first, they even built chimneys out of wood, and lined them with clay. This choice of materials, combined with thatch roofs, led to a

An heirloom porcelain tea set, a wing chair, and an ancestral portrait evoke New England ambiance. The stenciled border is an easily replicated regional note.

great many fires in settlers' communities, so that as early as 1627 thatch roofs and wooden chimneys were outlawed.

The fireplace, used for cooking as well as a source of warmth and light, continued to dominate rooms. With gigantic swinging iron cranes to hold cooking pots, they were kept blazing day and night. The mantle shelves were crowded with a few treasured books, highly burnished pewter plates, a handy musket, and other items. Sleeping lofts seldom had a fireplace, so most time was spent in the all-purpose keeping room, where family members said prayers, cooked, ate, spun, wove, sewed, read, and slept. Close to the heart of New England homes were high-backed wooden benches with arms, called settles. Cushioned with loose pillows covered in needlework, these early sofas helped to deflect drafts. An ensemble of fireplace and settle, perhaps a pierced tin lantern, and a spinning wheel creates an image that resonates with the home life of an era when virtually the entire family toiled incessantly to contribute to survival.

As the colonies developed and the economy diversified, the keeping room gave way to a variety of specialized rooms.

The most decorative, formal, and least used of the new spaces was the great hall or parlor. It was different from living rooms today, because it was

18

© E. Silva/FPG International

Romney Cotton Print courtesy Brunschwig & Fils

still a multipurpose space, a place to hold weddings, christenings, banquets, receptions for important guests, and funerals. In such a room the focal fireplace wall was often highlighted with costly painted paneling up to the ceiling. Along the other side of the room paneling went only up to about waist height to form a wainscot.

We often imagine New England houses of the early 1700s, neatly grouped around the village common or close to a winding country lane, as painted white with green shutters and a picket fence. Actually, New Englanders didn't routinely start to paint the exteriors of their houses until about the time of the Revolutionary War. It's still possible in Deerfield, Massachusetts, to see weathered brown or gray houses dating from that period without a trace of paint. In contrast to the unpainted exteriors, however, paint was used quite liberally to enhance interiors and embellish furniture. The seventeenth-century House of Seven Gables, in Salem, Massachusetts, with tiny lead-framed casement windows and dark rooms, is a famous example of a typical early New England home. The Puritans, with their notorious witch trials, seem to us the very personification of cheerless, repressed prudes with dark clothes and rooms alike. Once life regained some semblance of order and ceased to be an unrelenting struggle for sur-

OPPOSITE PAGE: *Although pine woodwork was usually painted in the seventeenth and eighteenth centuries, the stripped and waxed boards of this New England style hall, with its narrow stair, add a mellow warmth that is welcoming to the visitor. Although the sage green trim of the dining room beyond is correct for the early eighteenth century, the large windows would only have existed after the 1740s.*

ABOVE: *A reproduction of a block-printed cotton originally made in England in 1867.*

19

On a private street in New York's Greenwich Village, interior designer Timothy Van Dam has recreated an environment that exudes the cozy quality of New England rooms. Furniture is grouped around the fireplace, the ceiling beams have been left exposed, and the floor is covered by oriental rugs. The unlined muslin curtains with striped silk valances used in conjunction with venetian blinds are a practical and decorative window treatment typical of the late eighteenth-century.

20

vival, colonists eagerly sought to brighten their homes with vivid colors and interesting textures. Contemporary accounts and portraits reveal that colonists were partial to using sensual silks, warm velvets, and brilliant embroideries in their decor. Indeed, so popular were these rich fabrics that the authorities of the time passed laws to curtail such luxurious comfort and vainglorious display. These laws were doomed to failure. Given an opportunity, even humble folk opted for rich hues, using a myriad of unlikely colorants: copper powder for a vibrant blue-green, iron dust for a rich, red-brown, and cow urine for yellow, to make paint. Like Mario Buatta and many other modern interior designers, they realized that a resonant color is probably the cheapest, easiest way to bring a room to life. The actual colors of the painted woodwork were a lot more robust than what we might expect after seeing the subtle tones to which old furniture and paneling have faded in museums. These bright colors were echoed in geometric and floral motifs painted on furniture and embroidered on and woven into fabric.

The rainbowlike color schemes of these rooms must have produced a mellow glow when lighted

by the leaping hearth flames. Because candles were costly, few were in use for everyday purposes. Movies set in that period that show dozens of candles ablaze in rooms with no people in them are not very accurate. Such waste would never have occurred, even in the richest of households. Most of the time a couple of candles—four to six at the most—were considered sufficient to light a room. Only for gala entertaining or celebrations were chandeliers lighted. Indeed, whenever someone lighted more than ten candles in one room, people were impressed and commented upon the event in their diaries and letters! Artificial illumination, whether by candles, whale oil, or kerosene lamps, was considered extremely costly in New England from the seventeenth to the nineteenth centuries. To capitalize on the available light sources in a room, New Englanders introduced reflective materials and polished surfaces wherever they could. Shimmering brass, copper, and pewter were used for andirons, locks, drawer pulls, and lighting implements. Such bright touches were greatly prized. In time, silver, made into all sorts of useful objects, also became fashionable. In the days before banks, silver had the additional advantage of

© Robert Perron

© Bill Rothschild/interior design by Marilyn Rose

FAR LEFT: *Neoclassical style ceiling ornaments (once only available in plaster, now reproduced in resin, fiberglass, or embossed paper) impart a sense of elegance.*

LEFT: *The robustly carved woodwork of an early 1930s house, designed by the great American architect William Lawrence Bottomley, accentuates the English inspired decor flavored by eighteenth-century Yankee aristocrats. Using floral chintz, Chippendale chairs, and paired Chinese Export porcelains and paintings, designer Marilyn Rose has captured a look once only possible through inheritance.*

enabling one to keep an eye on the family wealth and impress guests at the same time. Some of the most lovely and sought-after antique American silver was hand-wrought in the great port city of Boston by artisans like the patriot Paul Revere.

TRADITIONAL NEW ENGLAND STYLE

Like many of his prosperous contemporaries, Paul Revere had his likeness recorded for posterity in a portrait. The artist of this renowned work was John Singleton Copley. Portraits remain key components in New England decorating. Through the use of inherited furniture, silver, and especially portraits, rooms in New England often take on the appearance of familial temples. The only rivals to these ancestral shrines are similar rooms found in the American South. Both are characterized by elaborate decors, virtually indistinguishable from their British counterparts. The resemblance to aristocratic English rooms is, of course, not accidental.

It has been said of Boston and a few other New England towns that they are cousins of London and Bath with their dignified residences of red brick. By the turn of the nineteenth century, during the so-called Federal period of design, rural and town houses were distinguished by the use of brick in town and wood only in the country. This brought about the second great type of New England room. Influenced by the brilliant Scottish architect and designer Robert Adam, who was famous for his study of Roman architecture newly discovered at Pompeii and Herculaneum, Yankee architects like Charles Bulfinch and Samuel McIntyre popularized the Neoclassical style. For the first time, New England rooms were differentiated by contrasting shapes. There were oval salons with niches and octagonal rooms with arched windows. Painted paneling all but disappeared in favor of architraves, or surrounds, with pilasters and cornices for doors and windows. Walls might be papered, often with panoramic scenes of landscapes from around the world, or of Roman ruins. The wallpapers, printed with wooden blocks, were produced at France's Zuber and duFors factories. By 1802, wallpaper was printed in the United States.

© Nancy Hill/Courtesy House Beautiful Home Remodeling & Decorating

OPPOSITE PAGE: *Jigsaw fretwork graces a mid-nineteenth century cottage on Martha's Vineyard.*

LEFT: *Exuberant Victorian pattern against pattern is used by decorator Anne Mullin along with New England heirlooms in an unrestrained example of late Northeastern Style.*

23

The British Adam style was not only promoted by local architects, it was also made familiar to potential builders and carpenters in pattern books brought to America from England. The style spread also through the use of ornamentation cast out of paste called composition that was mass-produced here and in England. Delicate garlands, ribbons, and urns in the latest style could be used even by farmers to decorate ceilings and mantle pieces. When painted, these embellishments were undetectable from hand-crafted work.

Trade was an important factor in the progressive sophistication of New England rooms. Cut glass and chandeliers were imported from Ireland, books and furniture from England, and mirrors and porcelain from France. All these fabulous luxuries from abroad have their place in today's New England rooms as well. Undoubtedly, though, the objects that identify these rooms with the golden age of New England are those originating in the Orient. There is scarcely a New England family of any repute that doesn't possess some trinket linked to the China Trade.

"Export porcelains" produced in Canton for export to Europe and America deliberately imitated china made in England and France. Some of the most exquisite examples of these enormous dinner services are valued for their rich, lustrous "orange rind" surfaces. A variety of designs were available, of which the most famous was probably the blue and white willow motif, said to tell the story of doomed lovers fleeing a jealous king. They died together at the end of the story and were transformed into birds. George Washington had a set of export porcelain made to his own pattern, depicting a trumpeting figure of "fame personified." Special colors, monograms, and coats of arms were also popular. The Chinese artisans were exceedingly clever and could imitate Western silver and other products as well. However, the more exotic items, including silk, jade, lacquer screens, boxes, trays, and ivory, were in greater demand. Tea was another extremely popular import from the Far East. Some frugal New Englanders even used the gold and silver foil paper that lined tea boxes to paper the walls of their drawing rooms.

Following the Civil War, the decline of trade and the proliferation of factory-made furniture, wallpaper, and accessories caused New England rooms to steadily lose their characteristic flair. They

RIGHT: **Willow ware and other old patterns of blue and white ironstone have long been treasured in New England homes.**

BELOW: **Do not overlook the decorative possibilities of a seashell or of apples in a Native American basket.**

24

came to resemble Victorian rooms elsewhere in the country, their heritage suggested only by the occasional inclusion of portraits, old silver, heirloom furniture, oriental carpets, and Chinese bric-a-brac crowded amongst the typical matching suite of furniture. Nevertheless, today New England has some of the country's most handsome Victorian and early twentieth-century eclectic residential architecture which, like the original New England homes, boast remarkable regional rooms.

DOWN EAST STYLE

Even a quick glance at the homes of upper New England — Vermont, New Hampshire, and Maine — reveals qualities unique to the region. "Big house, little house, back house, barn" is not, as you might think, a local nursery rhyme. Instead, it describes a residential style marked by rambling construction, in which house, barn, woodshed, pump house, and every other sort of outbuilding imaginable are

strung together. Anyone who has visited these states between October and May will appreciate the wisdom of the year-round residents in using this arrangement of their buildings. They inventively avoid having to spend any length of time outside during the winter. There are many fine historic houses in south New England that share the four-square layout, traditionally with two rooms on either side of a center hall. However, in most regional examples along the northern frontier, this conventional plan breaks out in a series of wings, ells, and lean-to sheds.

Stoves and fireplaces naturally assumed important roles in these homes. Even today many upper New Englanders eschew oil or gas furnaces in favor of heating their spaces with individual wood stoves. However, most of the old-fangled cast-iron stoves have been replaced by fuel-efficient, high-tech wonders. From the decorative standpoint, this is a great pity. Early nineteenth-century stoves, sometimes shaped into fantastic forms such as a classical lyre or an archway, occasionally topped by a patriotic eagle, are quite beautiful. In fact, even the

Crisp white woodwork contrasted with painted or papered walls lends distinction to many simple Down East rooms.

25

plain, oblong, vernacular iron stoves, on high, skinny legs have a certain streamlined grace.

At Vermont's superlative Shelburne Village Restoration and Museum of American Crafts, there are many excellent examples of both types of stoves. This enormous collection, once derided as kitchen furniture and American junk, contains a wide variety of unique regional elements. The collection showcases the full extent of native New England decorative genius. If the culture to the South was preoccupied with replicating English aristocratic environments, that of the North was focused on adapting the traditional lifestyle to a cold climate. The oil lamps, patchwork quilts, glass, pottery, and decoys that furnished Down East houses are all on view in the Shelborne Museum—these elements of the past may prove inspirational to those seeking to recreate the charm of a simpler time in their home decor.

Particularly fascinating are scrimshaw objects. These pieces, made from "Yankee ivory" (whalebone or walrus ivory), reflect Maine's importance during the first half of the nineteenth century as a center of ports. The China Trade of the Clipper ships made the fortunes of Boston and Providence, but Augusta, New Bedford, and New London became boomtowns because of the whale oil bonanza of the 1830s and '40s. The newly prosperous built grand Greek Revival style residences. From the squat "monitor" cupolas and railed "widow's walk" platforms set atop the roofs of their mansions, women searched the horizon for the return of the ships on which their men had sailed. Meanwhile, during the long hours spent at sea, sailors carefully carved and engraved whale's teeth

One of the tremendous pleasures of living in or visiting the Northeast is its abundant historic architecture, which brings the past into the present. Many of the early American entrepreneurs who made fortunes in the China trade and from whaling built Greek Revival mansions in the region.

26

© William Gross

and bones into such items as yarn-collecting reels, fans, and decorated corset stays as presents for their loved ones.

By the time of the Civil War, the whaling era was over. Kerosene replaced whale oil for lamp fuel and a great epoch ended abruptly. Scrimshaw gives Down East regional rooms an accent as unmistakable as the no-nonsense clipped speech of the area, perhaps best illustrated by Vermont's Calvin Coolidge. Once approached by a nervous lady who announced, "Mr. President, I've just bet I can get you to say more than three words," Coolidge quickly replied, "You lose."

A similar economic approach was used to decorate Down East interiors. Spacious rooms, unencumbered by a lot of superfluous "stuff," were

Port Royal courtesy Brunschwig & Fils

© Jeff Greenberg

painted in bright, clear yellows and brilliant reds with crisp white woodwork. Such color would give a room a sunny aspect even on a cloudy day. Dainty dotted Swiss or ball-fringed cotton curtains heightened this sunny illusion. Like the Scandinavians before them, Down-Easters have long used double glazing in their windows and avoided openings entirely on northern exposures. Fiercely independent, the Down-Easters have long had a reputation for great frugality. They also had a lot of time to spare over the long, cold winter, so hardly a household, at least in the rural regions, ever needed store-bought, machine-made curtains, carpets, or quilts.

Wide-board floors, painted duck-egg blue and dotted here and there with rag and braided rugs or, better still, some of the prettiest hooked rugs in the country, were the order of the day. Rugs depicting dogs and flowers are still made, and decorate the Down East retreats of some of the summer residents. On the subject of purchasing regional crafts and furniture, "Don't be fooled now," warns a shrewd native, "because there are many things, from painted chairs to butter churns, still made in northern climes just the same way as they always were. The best baskets, wooden boxes, quilts, and such are not inexpensive, but they're peanuts compared to what those city summer folk pay for an old wore-out or roughed-up one."

MID-ATLANTIC STYLE

Houses featuring exuberant Victorian rooms, shaded by louvered inside shutters or wraparound verandas are as traditional to Harlem and Saratoga, New York, and Cape May, New Jersey, as frankfurters and saltwater taffy are to Coney Island and Atlantic City. The style of the entire Mid-Atlantic region exudes a turn-of-the-century ambience in the same way that New England recalls the Colonial period. Historically, as New England's economic boom waned following the Civil War, the Mid-Atlantic region became an industrial force.

This isn't to say that there are no great antebellum Mid-Atlantic Rooms. There are many, inside fieldstone and shingled houses, revealing a distinct Dutch or German heritage. These houses usually had English architectural embellishments in addition to those borrowed from the continent. Thick inside shutters, doors divided in half to promote breezes but keep out livestock, hooded fireplaces lined with Delft tiles, and German ceramic woodstoves are but a few of the interior features associated with the Dutch Colonial style of New Amsterdam and the Pennsylvania Dutch (Deutsche, or German) style.

ABOVE: *The highly organized divisions of the classical architecture of early America that pervades the Northeast is so beautiful that great quantities of furniture oftentimes are made to seem superlative. The juxtaposition of strong color against white—whether on the walls or woodwork—adds vitality to finely articulated spaces.*

ABOVE LEFT: *This print was adapted from an Axminster rug in the Winterthur Museum.*

FOLLOWING PAGE: *Steep mansard roofs with fishscale slates, bracketed eaves, canted bay windows, and most importantly, a wraparound veranda, imbue Cape May's Gibson House with the hallmarks of post-Civil War era Mid-Atlantic style.*

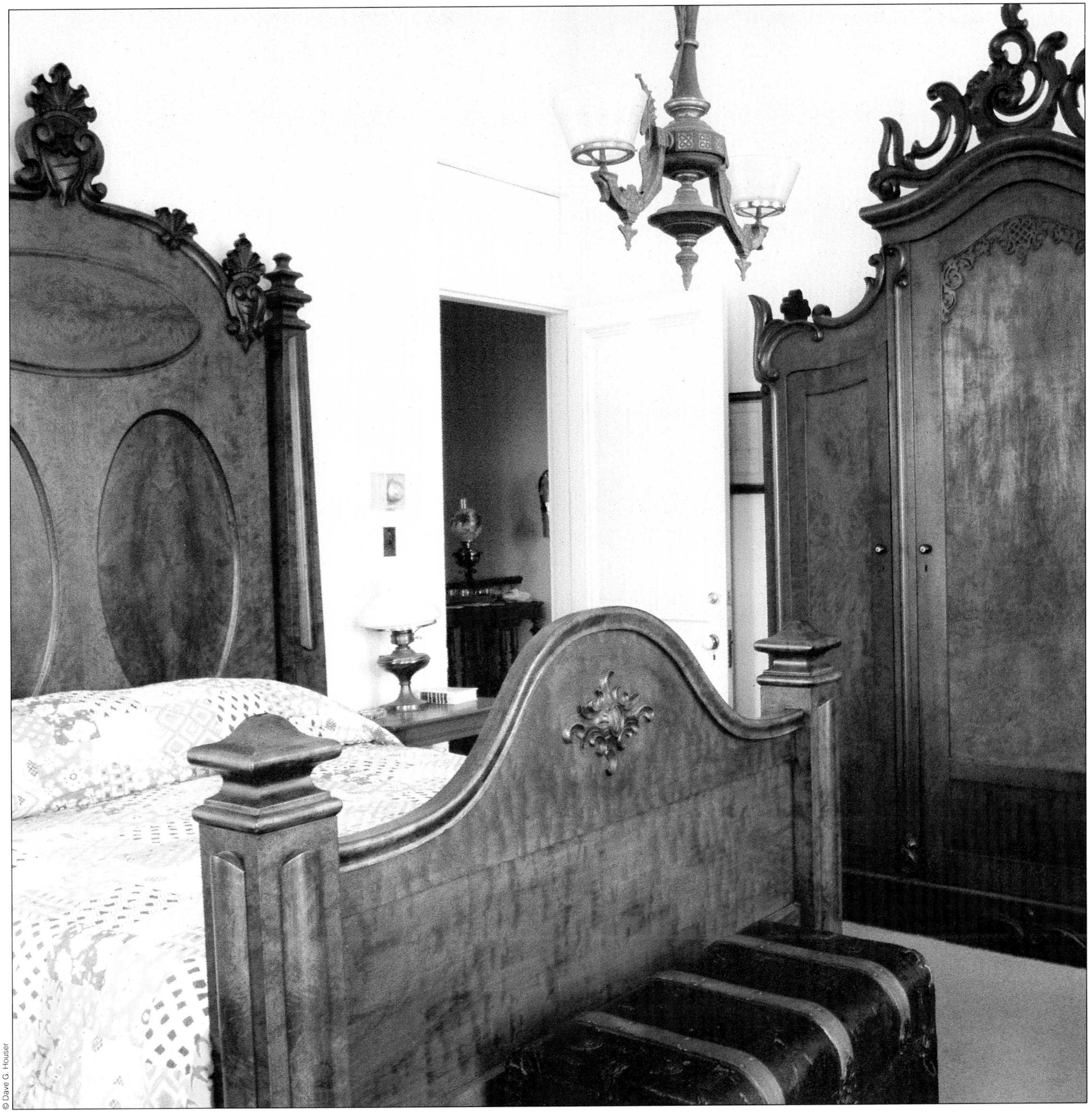

© George Goodwin

PRECEDING PAGE: *An elaborate suite of massive Victorian bedroom furniture in figured mahogany welcomes guests at Cape May's Main Stay Inn.*

ABOVE: *Lyndhurst, at Tarrytown, New York, is America's most extraordinary surviving Gothic Revival mansion. Designed by Alexander J. Davis and built in sections between 1838 and 1864, it was home to the Paulding, Merritt, and Gould families.*

Ultimately, English design trends, including the Neoclassical and Gothic Revival modes, overshadowed traditional ethnic styles of decoration. By the 1880s the Victorian taste for opulent, cluttered interiors, with rich, somber, pattern-on-pattern textures and exotic Oriental accessories, was all the rage in the urban centers and fashionable suburbs of the Mid-Atlantic region. To the modern way of thinking, the gorgeous, highly contrasted, even melodramatic decorating effects beloved by the Victorians may sometimes seem overdone. Many historians, though, are amazed at how strongly the look popular one hundred years ago is reminiscent of fashionable decorating today.

The prevailing prosperity of the Mid-Atlantic produced two schools of interior design that remain equally expressive of the area's style. Around the turn of the century, in the posh suburbs along the

Hudson River and the Pennsylvania Railroad Main Line, at Greenwich, Connecticut, and Locust Valley, Long Island, the well-to-do built gracious homes imitating English Tudor manor houses, Italian Renaissance villas, and French chateaux. Many of these houses, dating from about 1890 to 1930, with rooms full of antique and reproduction European and American furniture, are now considered historic landmarks. Built on a grandiose scale, featuring marble fireplaces, gilded bronze chandeliers, stained-glass windows, and hand-carved wood paneling, their likes will probably never be built again. These houses are now being lovingly restored and decorated in the original styles. Yet there is another side to Mid-Atlantic decorating that is considerably less traditional.

This school, which believes that anything new is inherently better than anything old, gave

With a wallpaper frieze depicting stylistic peacocks, quartersawn oak woodwork, and a bottle glass window, the inglenook of the 1880s Turner House represented the stylistic cutting edge of its era.

rise to the Art Nouveau (late nineteenth century), Art Deco (1920s and '30s), and High-tech (mid-twentieth century) movements. In the fast paced big cities of the Mid-Atlantic, there has always been a profound appreciation of the cutting edge. The urban passion for the avant garde has led to the creation of many remarkable rooms, which perfect-ly captured the moment when they were designed and yet are now as passé as dinosaurs. Time capsules, they are at once entirely out of fashion and excitingly new. Such rooms speak not only of the past but also of the future. This is the sophisticated urban regional room, a tradition in large cities throughout the country.

Designing Northeastern Rooms

LEFT: *The paisley patterned dust ruffle and hangings on a fourposter bed (so high that it requires a step) add to the intimate atmosphere of this low-ceilinged Down East style bedroom.*

ABOVE: *This fabric, adapted from a mid-nineteenth-century damask, lends a historical touch typical of the traditional Northeastern room.*

33

There are at least four approaches to achieving regional ambience and decor. I'll only seriously speak of three, though. Of the fourth I will say only that if you are prepared to spend copiously, consider seeking professional assistance. Interior designers, architects, landscape gardeners, and art and antiques consultants can do it all for you. This method of creating a home environment has certain advantages, not the least of which is that there's always someone else to blame when things go wrong. For most people, though, it's a rather impersonal, detached, and boring way to go about decorating a home. Professionals are invaluable because their experience, expertise, and resources can help you avoid all sorts of unfamiliar pitfalls. There is really no substitute, though, for the thrill of putting it all together yourself. If you take the time to haunt antique shops, garage and house sales, and flea markets, somewhere you'll find that perfect something for a fraction of the cost of an identical example you saw advertised in *Architectural Digest* or *HG*.

Oakley Cotton & Linen Print courtesy Brunschwig & Fils

ABOVE: *A painted hanging shelf with turned containers, a splendid ladder-back chair, and a rough brick floor illustrate the simplicity of Down East decor. If you try too hard to get fancy, you won't get it right.*

ABOVE RIGHT: *Reproduction of an English wallpaper dated 1856.*

OPPOSITE PAGE: *The soft glow of light from a ceiling fixture with a ruffled shade enhances New England antiques displayed against a dull red background in a room designed by David Parker.*

34

You might sometimes have to factor in the cost of repairing a broken door or leg, but it's still worth it if you like the piece. Perhaps it won't fit the space you originally envisioned, but don't worry—for a good piece of furniture, you can always find a place. You may even come to adore the thrill of discovering bargain treasures. A new coat of paint, a few repairs, even making holes to accommodate a television set or sink can all be undertaken without the guilty feeling that you've defiled a masterpiece. So when you feel envious of multibillionaires and their fabulous antiques, remember that they probably haven't had so very much to do with the formation of the over-rich, over-perfect spaces they inhabit. Too often they view the art on their walls and antiques in their rooms as mere investments. Seldom do they know the satisfaction of the investment of time, thought, and imagination that transforms objects into precious memories and talismans.

Having said all this, it is nonetheless very important to *always* buy the best quality you can afford. This rule is particularly appropriate when dealing with big items, from a house or apartment to a piano or sofa. Ornaments and smaller pieces of furniture can be of lesser quality but still provide excellent decorative or diversionary value. However, this is seldom true of the big stuff.

NEW ENGLAND

You've decided you want a New England room. If you were to seriously consider the authentic reproduction of such spaces, the tremendous expense of acquiring the genuine old elements necessary for authenticity would undoubtedly give you cause to pause. Recently, for instance, a less-than-exceptional American poplar corner cupboard, circa 1830, with original sky-blue and butter-yellow paint, sold at auction for just under $20,000. This, of course, was just a single piece of furniture. Given this daunting fact, you may feel defeated before you've even started, but you really mustn't give up so easily!

Rich or poor, New Englanders have traditionally abhorred the very notion of having to purchase anything new. Not unlike the old English aristocracy, they found venerable objects, especially inherited ones, vastly superior to the shiny new examples found in stores. These values are generally the exact opposite of much popular sentiment today. However, if you appreciate the romance of owning the very objects that have sustained your ancestors, you can readily create stylishly "shabby-chic" New England rooms.

As mentioned before, portraits are salient elements of New England interiors. If you haven't

35

36

Portraits, china, and silver are essential for recalling high-style New England interiors.

inherited any, don't despair. From old photographs of family members, local portrait artists can often achieve a remarkable likeness. Then again, if you have your own progeny, you might consider having current family portraits painted. In each case, an affordable artist to preserve your likeness or venerate those of your relatives can probably be found at the art department of the closest university. Alternately, unless they're the work of famous painters, other people's family portraits can be obtained quite cheaply at house sales. You really ought not to give a second thought to knowing the identity of the lady in the black velvet hooped skirt. Guests will assume that she and other portraits, especially those of less-than-beautiful subjects, are your ancestors. Why else would you have them? Well, the other reason is to create a certain atmosphere, to suggest with those frozen images from the past a certain continuity, an association with all that was

excellent long ago. In this way, portraits suggest "a comforting sense of security and permanence," says historian Chippy Irvine. "As any duke will tell you, not recalling who the people in your portraits are is irrelevant. This ignorance in no way diminishes their ability to cast a spell of the good old days that never were, which is the ultimate function of the painted image."

House sales can be the source of much more than portraits. Monogrammed or crested silver, china, and linens are also very expressive of New England regional rooms. Many a dowager with more daughters than sets of family China Trade porcelain has surreptitiously acquired an extra dinner service for the latest wedding—at a house sale. The fact that monograms, coats of arms, or portraits can't be placed by the present generation simply emphasizes the extent of good family connections. So comb those sales, make good deals,

Le Verger D'abondance courtesy Brunschwig & Fils

© Balthazar Korab

paint, repair, and recover when necessary, and combine well-made reproductions or simple modern pieces that fade into the background. This recipe is guaranteed to provide you with old-fashioned elegance. To recall the topical flavor of New England, add those special piquant touches indigenous to the region. For example, collect Sandwich glass in a kaleidoscope of vibrant hues. It is still manufactured in Massachusetts today. The golden-colored glass is especially beautiful when a collection is displayed in a bow-fronted or curved bay window. It also looks nice with blue and white ceramics—whether Chinese, Delft, or Majolica.

Golden yellow, cobalt blue, and soft, almost gray, oyster white is a classic New England color combination. Pumpkin orange, emerald green, and lilac mauve were also frequent choices for adorning the pine-paneled trim of quaint chambers. Often, a harmonious variant—a lighter tint or darker shade of the room's dominant color of paint or wallpaper—was used as the trim and floor color. "The colonists and their early descendants knew what they were doing," explains veteran interior designer Terry McQuan. "They weren't made to suffer the confusing choices we have now. They'd employ a single wall color, augmented by curtains and upholstery in subordinant tones. Sometimes a contrasting tape or ribbon border or trimming was used. Otherwise,

though, both harmonious and complementary accents were introduced rather selectively."

Fortunately, a number of companies supply scenic, architectural, and boldly patterned papers appropriate to New England·homes, and an equal number mix authentic paint colors. There are a variety of New England standbys that have never been out of production, including Cape Cod candles and baskets, Chickering pianos, patchwork quilts, Hitchcock chairs, and rag rugs, both braided and hooked. There are also excellent reproductions of New England antiques available. Museum shops and catalogs, from Deerfield to Chester, sell finely made replicas of objects from their collections. Some are so good that they've taken in experts. Finally, national furniture manufacturers have specific New England–inspired lines to lend a regional flavor to any room.

Replicating a museum room is the goal many people wish to achieve in a New England room. By deliberately juxtaposing New England elements and colors, such as stencils or splattered floors, and the occasional set-piece antique, with contemporary furniture, architecture, or both, a decorator can bring the New England regional room up to date. Though it is not the look for those who want to conjure up the past, it can produce dynamic effects. New York designer Timothy Van Dam sug-

ABOVE: *A child's quilt and local wood carvings, including one that depicts a unicorn chained to a tree, instill this room with regional appeal.*

ABOVE LEFT: *This fabric, adapted from a nineteenth-century tapestry, lends a historical feeling to a room.*

37

The Empire style candelabrum, Staffordshire china figures of royalty, and, of course, the magnificent gilded harp represent a sampling of the European imports used to decorate New England rooms.

38

tural components in a room to create a focal point." These elements might range from colorful carousel horses to massive pine hutches and dressers for displaying pewter and china, or even for storing television sets, VCRs, and stereo equipment. A block-fronted mahogany breakfront bookcase loaded with Morocco-bound volumes would also fit the bill of a New England prop. Essentially, the pristine, hard, shiny aesthetic of high-tech is diametrically opposed to the soft, warm, mature comfort of New England regional rooms—but it's exactly that complex combination and, sometimes, confrontation of old and new in impressionistic interiors that make them so exciting!

gests that "when you want the best of all possible worlds, the best of the past and the finest of today's modern furniture, it's a good idea to find impressive architectural antiques and use them as if they were sculptures. By impressive I mean big, substantial pieces of furniture. In fact, you can even use elements of the architecture, like a massive column in a loft, or an elaborate wooden staircase, as sculp-

DOWN EAST

Don't rather than *do* is the operative word when creating an authentic Down East interior. Don't overdo anything is the most important rule of this region's style. If it is possible to get by without repainting, for instance, a Down-Easter would advise using "a little soap and water and let it be." This is an excellent recommendation for old houses and furniture alike. Sometimes a timeworn piece marred by a blistered or flaking finish and

© Lynton Gardiner

Blue and white was probably the most popular color combination used Down East in the past. This pleasant guest room with rag rugs and a faux bamboo bed show that it's still a viable choice.

covered in dirt or even mold will emerge from a thorough scrubbing to reveal a lovely color and patina. Be sure to use a soft brush and a mild cleaning agent. If you suspect that an object is truly valuable, seek professional advice about the best method for refurbishing it. In most cases, however, you'll find that a simple cleaning can work wonders.

Not surprisingly, the next important Down East don't to consider is, Do not replace. If you have a beloved quilt, slipcover, or curtains that have become worn about the edges with use, you can stitch on a contrasting tape, ribbon, fringe, or other trimming to hide the wear, holes, and tears. This applied border may first require a wash in tea or a diluted commercial dye so that the old and new material will not be glaringly distinguishable. It is also possible to reglaze old chintzes, which further prolongs the material's life. Although salespeople are often correct when they estimate that to reupholster an old chair or sofa, or even to make a new slipcover, will cost almost as much as a new piece of furniture, they often neglect to mention that the new chair or sofa will undoubtedly be of a lesser quality than the one you already own. Down East Yankees like architect Charles A. Platt feel absolutely certain of this. "We could never find a couch as comfortable or with quite the perfect shape that our old one has," says the Cornish, New Hamp-

shire, resident. You might feel that same way about your own tried and true piece of furniture. If it is well made from high quality materials you'll be forever grateful if you decide to restore rather than to replace it.

Down East don'ts for curtains and upholstery: Don't use velvet, silk, or brocaded fabric. Do use primitive pattern chintzes for upholstering and blocked linen, organdy, dotted swiss, and gingham curtains. Likewise, gilded furniture, fine porcelain, delicate soap-bubble thin glassware, elaborate silver, and crystal chandeliers are inappropriate accents. Instead, use pewter, gaily colored pottery, pressed glass, and baskets. Either bright or pale walls with contrasting woodwork complete the feeling of a rural, open, bright, and unfussy Down East regional room.

Utility and simplicity are the most sought-after qualities in a Down East setting. A marble fireplace mantle would be out of place, but rough-hewn pine shelves above a fire surround of old irregular brickwork or delft tiles would be perfect. Paring down, requiring the exercise of great restraint, is more difficult than elaboration. In a simple room, the eye is more critical of isolated objects, which in cluttered surroundings would be less noticeable. Despite their modesty, Down East rooms are full of subtle pleasures: the beauty of fine lines, the contrast of

bold patterns, and the gratification of seeing materials worked in such a way as to fully reveal their natural qualities. The texture of a glaze, the grain of walnut, the intense glimmering of colored glass in the sunlight—these are the uncomplicated, yet profound, satisfactions of the Down East room.

ABOVE: *The Mid-Atlantic's collecting craze is exemplified by a shelf of cookie jars in the dining room of art dealer Hal Bromm.*

FAR RIGHT: *An endless collection of globes and books provides infinite points of interest in the New York apartment of stylemakers Suzanne Slesin and Michael Steinberg. "Kids, friends, and family—everyone gets into the act when you're starting to collect things. To me it's no fun if you collect something that everyone else collects or if the objects cost a lot of money."*

40

MID-ATLANTIC STYLE

The Joy of Collecting

Abundance is both the blessing and the curse of the bustling cities of the Mid-Atlantic. As a result, there are almost too many options to choose from when you set out to make a Mid-Atlantic space. The two basic approaches or prevailing tastes have been characterized as all out, old world–inspired opulence or all out, New Age–inspired avant garde. Collections have come to be essential to both styles. Because of the high concentration of decorators, suppliers, antique shops, auction houses, flea markets, and thrift stores, collecting has become more mania than simple hobby for most Mid-Atlantic residents. So whatever your taste, whether it be for sybaritic splendors or modern mannerism, a

42

OPPOSITE PAGE: *In Philadelphia, interior designer George Wallace brings the Mid-Atlantic opulent look up to date with a gold ceiling and striped paint job on the walls as a setting for English Regency chairs and Chinese ceramics.*

RIGHT: *In the author's tiny apartment, a sumptuous effect is achieved with hand-me-down Mario Buatta curtains and thrift shop finds. Pencil drawings on the walls provide additional interest.*

collection of treasured objects can give your environment the "hip-haute" East Coast look.

A collection need not consist of precious or even pretty objects. The collections of New York style setter Suzanne Slesin are an excellent case in point. Globes of the world and solar system, state souvenir plates, and even 1950s and '60s "ugly vases," of which Ms. Slesin enthuses "they're so mundane that they're brilliant," are just three of the collections that ensure that no matter where she might travel, she has an object to seek. A more common passion is the love of books, which figure prominently and in profusion in many Mid-Atlantic homes. For the unorthodox, though, there are transistor radios, old shoes, cookie jars— such a collection can transform an anonymous high-rise flat or any other unimaginative raw space into a home with Mid-Atlantic style. Indulge your sense of fantasy and start to collect.

MID-ATLANTIC

Opulence

A famous dealer in Old Masters is said to have recited to clients the ditty: "Little sticks of Ivory, precious bit of Boulle, harmonize with Venuses of

Boldly marblized wallpaper dramatizes an inexpensive plaster bust in the library of a New York loft. Woodgrain-painted tin boxes are displayed on the bookshelf.

44

the Flemish school." This amusing verse reflects the wide range and consistent high quality of antiques and collectibles to be found in the Mid-Atlantic region. With such a profusion of choices, discipline is always the key to making a myriad of diverse objects form a pleasing and unified room. A

strongly architectural setting makes an ideal starting point. Alas, many modern houses tend to be devoid of architectural character. Architecture needn't be Neoclassical or revivalist in style in order to define a space. All that's necessary is that it articulate, or visually reinforce, the overall space. Openings, such as windows and doors; projections, such as cabinets and fireplace mantles, and voids, such as niches and alcoves must all relate to one another in some way. Traditionally, the relationships among a room's elements and components were achieved mathematically. With various ratios of floor shape to wall height, for instance, architects devised and continually refined over the centuries a proportional system for achieving grace and beauty.

Just as an architect uses proportion to make a building and its parts orderly, so too a designer must use a system to keep control over the display of a collection. To avoid chaos, you must determine some means of relating items to each other and to their surroundings. Repetitions of objects of similar size and shape arranged in large groupings is the simplest means of regulating a collection. For example, arranged on identical shelves around the periphery of a room, a collection of one hundred teapots with the spouts all pointed in the same direction forms a rhythmically patterned backdrop that is more than just the sum of its parts.

© Alex McLean

The usual way to display a collection in a traditional Mid-Atlantic interior would be to use large case furniture: a breakfront chest, secretary, corner cabinets, hutch, or Welsh cupboard. A single room with a number of these pieces, even if they were from different stylistic periods, could be given a sense of coherent style if you covered the shelves and backs of each piece in fabric of the same color.

A profusion of visual elements is characteristic of Mid-Atlantic rooms, and it helps to create a sense of opulence. Pattern used against pattern is an important and alluring element of a grand Mid-Atlantic room. Color plays a leading role in the difficult game of using pattern on pattern. Some consistent reference is vital. For example, in a library with curtains made of a two-colored cut velvet, with red pomegranates against moss green, the background green might reemerge on a pleated

silken lampshade with a fringe of a deeper green. A mostly green seventeenth-century landscape tapestry placed behind a black damask sofa with crimson cushions might have an ancestral portrait hung against it. The portrait of a young woman wearing a pale blue dress with a scarlet sash hides a hole in the tapestry, which caused it to cost half of what it might have otherwise. In the same room, a Persian flower-garden-patterned carpet might have cream and blue flowers on a rose background. The trick of playing color and pattern—and size and shape—off one another is what gives Mid-Atlantic traditional rooms their coherence and fascination and saves these treasure troves from overwhelming with their complexity. Scale must never be forgotten, for one thing that is neither easy to find nor to afford in big Mid-Atlantic cities is an abundance of square footage.

In the same apartment shown on the previous page, the cream of an assemblage of faux bois tin boxes is displayed atop a late eighteenth-century continental chest of drawers made of pine but painted and grained to imitate tropical hardwoods.

RIGHT: *The soft green used for the walls was repeated on the back of this shelf in order to fully complement an arrangement of colorful majolica ware from the late-nineteenth century.*

BELOW: *Custom made shelves with a framework of copper tubing designed by Babette Holland display Suzanne Slesin's extensive collection of "ugly" 1950s vases.*

46

OPPOSITE PAGE: *The problem of an otherwise awkward top floor room with low sloping ceilings has been solved admirably by the use of a rich emerald carpet and paint on the walls and ceiling. This neutral treatment allows the exceptional Empire chair in the Neo-Egyptian style and other fine antiques to stand out uncontested.*

Every inch of these urban spaces must be made to do double duty when possible. For this reason the luxurious look of a tapestry-hung, book-lined, or tented room is immensely popular there. Not only do such rooms use as part of the decor objects that might otherwise require storage space, but they also allow for the construction of hidden cupboards and closets. Inexpensive cotton or rayon tenting can be made to look quite deluxe with the addition of a stitched-on border made of a double row of contrasting ribbon. Fabric-covered poles with tasseled cords surrounding the doors and windows can heighten the illusion of a tent pitched in some exotic place. If you design a tented bedroom or bathroom, closets can be built out on either side of the bed or bathtub to form an alcove. To alleviate a feeling of being too closed in, a mirror reflecting outward from parted draperies placed behind the bed or bathtub creates space while adding a touch of drama. This flourish can be reinforced by placing a mirror on the opposite wall, revealed from behind looped-back curtains. Usually closets are so needed that they are added to a room, but sometimes they are removed to create a small den or a guest bedroom. The doors and walls of a closet can be taken down, adding just enough space to a former dressing room to fit a single bed or two easy chairs. Lined in book shelves, drapery, painted murals, or mirrors, the room can be quite charming.

47

48

Dufrene Woven Damask courtesy Brunschwig & Fils

More than anything else, the process of creating the opulent style typical of the Mid-Atlantic (especially if you live in a city), requires imagination. It takes creativity and the ability to appreciate the complex relationships between spaces and the objects that occupy them.

MID-ATLANTIC

The Urban Cutting Edge

Of all regional styles, the Mid-Atlantic urban cutting-edge design and its sister, the Hollywood modern style, are most difficult to reinterpret authentically unless you are a creative artist yourself or you engage professional help. The modern style benefits very much from a dramatic drop-dead view or a lofty, clearly articulated space, neither of which may be readily available. It also requires boldness, theatrical lighting effects, and designer furnishings. These elements are neither inexpensive nor negotiable. However, this is an aesthetic in which less is definitely more. If anything could be said to differentiate the Mid-Atlantic cutting edge from its Los Angeles counterpart, it would in fact be the greater minimalism found in the East. Color is more subdued and materials are less obviously

OPPOSITE PAGE: *In this urbane environment, where everything has subdued tones with only a few spots of color provided by flowering plants, the spectacular view is the star.*

ABOVE: *Created by a French decorator in the 1920s, this opulent Art Deco print could be used to dramatic effect in a traditional Mid-Atlantic room.*

49

© Christopher Bain

RIGHT: *Black and white are used in this urban great room designed by Bruce Bierman to make everything, including the light fixtures and sprinkling pipes, into a patterned background for the artful explosion of color on one wall.*

BELOW: *If it's true that there is nothing more difficult to make interesting than a white room, it is equally true that no color is so festive and lively as regal red, especially in combination with black and white, as here, in the apartment of landscape designer and architect Kevin Wolfe.*

50

luxurious. For example, a popular countertop or bathroom material in New York is unpolished granite; in Hollywood houses, richly veined, polished marble and alabaster are popular. Similarly, muted tones of raw silk and soft leather are preferred in New York over the brightly colored shiny satin or exotic Far Eastern brocades typical of Los Angeles homes.

Like a Western interpretation of a Zen or Shinto-inspired room or garden, Mid-Atlantic cutting-edge rooms often treat the world outside as the focal point, with an entire room subordinate to a view from a window. A focal point inside the room might be an imposing fireplace or an important work of art. If your space lacks one of these elements, accentuate a feature that does exist. Look out the window: If a sea of skyscrapers or a range of mountains is in sight, don't hide them. On the other hand, if you look at a blank wall, add a group of plants requiring low light levels or a translucent screen of paper, cloth, or some sort of venetian blind. Interior shutters faced with mirrors are commonly found in grand salons of European palaces and make wonderful adjuncts to viewless windows. Opened on each side of a window banked with plants, they promote growth by intensifying what-

ever sunlight is available, and they make a room more bright by day. Closed at night and illuminated with uplight cans or overhead flood- or spotlights, they produce dazzling reflections of the plant leaves and weird exaggerated shadows.

If you are at all handy, you can make spotlights yourself. Tin coffee cans spray-painted black or white on the outside can easily be fitted with an electrical light socket. These can lights could be used either on the floor (up lights) or ceiling (down lights). For an extra finishing touch when they are used as ceiling lights, recess them up into the surface.

By placing a large piece of furniture diagonally in a corner, you can add a sculptural focus to a room otherwise lacking in architectural presence. So situated, even a piano could have a monumental effect. If a large window were nearby, the emphasis on the piano, desk, dressing table, or bed would be more pronounced. Diagonal placement in a corner is so effective because of its unexpectedness and unconventionality. Backed up by a decorative folding screen in brushed steel, lacquer, painted canvas, or mirrored panels, the cornerpiece irresistibly pulls the eye toward itself. A raised platform in a room—for a bed, sofa, dining table and chairs, or

objets d'art—also helps to focus attention. Sunken conversation pits are effective for centering a room but are more difficult to construct than platforms.

To further assure that your favorite work of art stands out you could use it as the basis for the room's color scheme. For example, if you have an abstract canvas with red as the predominating color, you could use contrasting colors, such as muted greens or blues, or harmonizing tones, colors derived from red, such as orange, violet, or pink. If you used these hues for upholstery, fabric, curtains, or rugs, then walls, ceiling, and floor would be best left in a neutral tone for the sake of balance and to achieve the minimalism and simplicity typical of Mid-Atlantic cutting-edge style.

You can also achieve a novel look by adapting ordinary materials to unusual uses. In the 1890s, innovative architect and designer Stanford White collected matchstick and split-bamboo shades, unfurled them and used them as wallpaper. In the living room of his Smithtown, Long Island, summer home he even used this matting on the ceiling. Sisal or straw matting could be used in a similar way to make a unique wall or floor covering. Photo murals, which were very much in vogue in the 1930s, are seldom seen today, yet they offer a host of exciting decorating possibilities. Black-and-white or hand-colored murals and unusual compositions

or montages can make an unusual and individual decorative statement.

The high cost of designer furniture, believe it or not, can sometimes be avoided by commissioning custom-made pieces. Fitted divans, tables, and beds can also save precious space in urban settings. Indeed, the streamlined efficiency to be achieved with built-in furniture and storage have always been a hallmark of avant garde design. Built-in pieces allow furniture to merge with background, creating the sense of spaciousness associated with the modern look. A decor that shows individual style and ingenuity is the goal of the Mid-Atlantic cutting edge.

Architect George Woo has subtly manipulated room levels and spatial volumes to create a secure red refuge in a lofty multipurpose environment.

51

Chapter Two

© Dick Dietrich

THE SOUTH

© Dick Dietrich

PRECEDING PAGE: *Doric columns and a graceful marble staircase continued to denote welcome in the South long after the Civil War, as in the gracious Oakwood Manor, built at the turn of the century in Franklin, Louisiana.*

ABOVE: *Embellished with a frieze of swirling acanthus leaves and Corinthian columns, the ballroom at Nottoway Plantation has been transformed into a space boasting the best of the past and present. Typical Victorian style floral patterned carpets, wallpaper, and heavy velvet draperies have been swept away, allowing architecture and a few select pieces of furniture to shine.*

Each year tens of thousands of eager tourists invade Southern cities like Charleston, Savannah, New Orleans, and Natchez in search of the past. They flock to the South not just for its poetic natural beauty but also for its unique ability to conjure up a way of life that faded long ago. Not just tourists, but Southerners themselves cherish these historic centers of high civility. They carefully preserve and restore virtually any physical relic from the time before "the War"—when cotton was king and tobacco, rice, sugar, and indigo were royal offspring. It is the completeness of Southerners' success in saving the region's vener-

able architecture in all its manifestations that enables visitors to fully appreciate the essence of the antebellum epoch.

Historical research will show that the charmed existence extolled in local lore was not as ideal as the pristine restorations at places like Williamsburg and elsewhere would seem to indicate. However, if you realize that these places have been slightly exaggerated to reach their present state of perfection, then you have come closer to understanding the secret ingredient of successful Southern regional rooms. Exaggeration and embellishment— enough for drama but not enough to cause

Even some smaller antebellum houses like the Fitzpatrick-Kelly place in Madison, Georgia, were ennobled by a classical portico.

55

vulgarity—this is the key to the authentic Southern regional room.

There are many stately mansions dating from before the Civil War in the northern and the midwestern regions of the United States. Few, though, are so magnificent as those in the South. Names such as Stratford Hall, Westover, Shirley, Drayton Hall, Gunston Hall, Gainswood, Bellevue, Oak Alley, and Longwood evoke the unmatched and irrefutable grandeur of Southern houses of this period. No small part of their dramatic presence was accomplished through exaggeration of scale and mass. Although many regions around the country boast fine Greek Revival residences with handsome porticos, the colonnaded houses of the South are more than mere dwellings. No less than the Parthenon is to Greece, they are shrines—to the familial glory and cultural accomplishment of the American South. In these houses the rooms are longer, the ceilings higher, and windows wider than almost any others in North America. This massive scale of course was a result of practical as well as aesthetic considerations. The sultry Southern climate is as famous as any other aspect of the region. It is used to explain the local pace—torturously slow or elegant in its leisure, depending on your point of view. It also explains the existence of lofty rooms shaded by verandas and cooled by scented breezes that

56

A dainty marble nymph is the highlight of the gently curving stairwell in Houmas House, in Louisiana.

tion owners with great satisfaction. Because hurricanes were not infrequent along the coast, the principal rooms with the most elaborate and costly decors were elevated to the first floor (in English terms) above the ground floor base of the house. This is how we derive the term *basement*, meaning ground floor, as distinct from an excavated cellar or undercroft.

From the street, the entrance led not into the interior but rather into the lower of the famous double veranda, piazza, or porch that was characteristic of the Charleston house. The double veranda, another feature borrowed from dwellings in the Caribbean, often overlooked a walled garden. The lower veranda at ground level served as a sort of outdoor waiting room for strangers and servants. Privileged guests were admitted into the hall and up the curving staircase to one of the upstairs drawing rooms.

Generally the drawing room was decorated in the latest English fashion, meaning imported furnishings and ornaments from France, Italy, and Britain, just as in the houses of prosperous Bostonians or New Yorkers. Houses throughout the North and the South during this period were furnished with excellent cabinetry supplied by talented regional furniture makers. Local taste and the particular styles of individual craftsmen led to

drift through the closed, louvered shutters of the exceptionally wide windows.

In Charleston, houses were finely adjusted to account for the weather. Wealthy planters spent the winter in their town residences following harvest, in a seasonal routine that some fortunate families continue to this day. Many early settlers in the Carolinas had lived previously in the West Indies or had West Indian trade connections. Not surprisingly, the tile-roofed, stuccoed-brick, one-room-deep dwellings of this equally torrid part of the world were adopted by the American planta-

© Dick Dietrich

© Dick Dietrich/FPG International

57

the development of specialized design characteristics that distinguished the furniture of one region from that of another. For example, at the end of the eighteenth century, Baltimore cabinetmakers used inlaid bellflower motifs in this way. They were also renowned for their virtuosity at incorporating églomisé, reverse painted glass panels usually depicting neoclassical subjects in black and gold, in their most ambitious pieces.

The wealthier citizens of New Orleans at this time used a great deal of imported furniture, primarily from France. However, something more than collections of Louis XV to Louis Napoleon furniture accounts for the cosmopolitan aura of this great seaport. Some of New Orleans's sophistication derives from its history of being passed back and forth between France and Spain until the Louisiana Purchase from Napoleon in 1804 made it part of the United States. Probably no other American city had received such diverse cultural contributions before the massive immigration wave of the 1890s. The first houses built in New Orleans during the eighteenth century were single-story, one-room-deep "shotgun houses," so called because it was said that a bullet could pass unobstructed from the front door through aligned interior room openings to the rear yard. For shade, covered porches ran across the facades of these homes. Ultimately,

the houses sat on high basements because of hurricanes and the propensity of low-lying New Orleans streets to flood. By the 1830s, it became fashionable to raise these porches higher still. Supported by slender columns, they became balconies set above covered public walkways. Lacelike cast-iron railings and piers adorned the balconies. Imported from northern foundries at New York and elsewhere, these highly ornamental railings have become one of New Orleans's most significant architectural features. Like the verandas at Savannah and the porticos of plantation houses, New Orleans's covered balconies were features developed in response to the climate—they allowed windows to be always left open—except during storms. And, of course, while open windows encouraged breezes, they also made mosquito netting essential on beds.

Also common in Southern homes, and equally important for ventilation, was the patio or courtyard, which had been a Spanish innovation. Lushly embowered with palmettos, crepe myrtle, and hibiscus, these open-air living rooms were often quite delightful with their greenery and gaily splashing fountains. However, the mosquitoes were sometimes so annoying that ladies sat inside a collapsible frame similar to a carriage roof, draped in more netting!

The substantial dignity of this mahogany four-poster bed in a small, low-ceilinged room of great modesty defies rules that say that small rooms require diminutive furniture. The tin tub, child's trundle bed, and rosette coverlet are all typically Southern reminders of the past.

58

© Dick Dietrich

The origin of certain elements of regional rooms is not always American, as we see with several aspects of Southern style. Punkas, heavy wooden fans originally found suspended from the center of the lofty ceilings of rooms in India, made their way here via England. In New Orleans, they were especially notable as a feature of dining rooms, where they were lazily pulled back and forth by servants. In an effort to avoid cooking smells and heat, kitchens in the South usually occupied structures totally separate from the main house. In New Orleans, in an attempt to keep the dining area at least within running distance of the kitchen, architects typically located dining rooms on the ground floor. Flood damage was kept to a minimum in these basement rooms by installing floors of tile brick or marble, inspired by floors in Venice.

© Mark E. Gibson

LEFT: *The humble honesty of log and newspaper-covered walls, a Singer sewing machine, and a plain patchwork quilt, often found in Southern cabins, are closer to the heritage and experience of many Americans than are the extravagant plantation houses.*

BELOW: *Hall trees are a staple feature in the homes of Southern grande dames.*

© Alex McLean

59

Southern rooms were also distinguished by the seasonal nature of their decor. In the spring, before folks abandoned town for seaside resorts and country estates, rooms were cleaned and given their summer dress or undress. Opulent, tasseled and fringed curtains of silk and velvet were removed to the attic cedar chest. Pile carpets were also taken up and supplanted by wall-to-wall straw matting. Seating pieces were covered in striped or floral cotton slipcovers, and beds were moved away from the walls in the line of breezes of cross ventilation. With the family's departure for the country, furniture, including pictures and chandeliers, was shrouded in muslin dust sheets and candles set into dishes of sand were set out to attract and burn dreaded moths.

Seasonal migrations by the rich were a great idea not only for people but also for regional rooms, which were given a yearly rest. Not everyone in the South could indulge in this luxury, however. Today, more than a few visitors to the restored mansions of the South, while appreciative of the beauty of their splendid rooms, find more to relate to in the humble habitations that once housed the slaves. In the slave quarters, discarded old-fashioned Queen Anne and Chippendale furniture, "too good to throw out," often stood in marked contrast to ladder-back and Windsor chairs and other variant types of spindle and turned furniture. Utterly unpretentious furniture of this sort was also found in the homes of the "small" farmers throughout the South. Their churns and looms, not to mention beds, tables, and chairs, possessed a unique beauty that derived from their inherent simplicity and utility. Slip- and salt-glazed pottery rivaled the most elegant translucent porcelain for imaginative and effective decoration. Increasingly rare stoneware jugs, made first by slaves and later by free blacks, often in the form of grotesque heads, are an especially apt example of artistic functionalism. So, too are all manner of pieced quilts, which, like the African-derived jugs, were made in most southern states. Found in log or board houses fronted with broad porches and roofed in shakes or tin, these modest mementos of the past resonate with the echoes of the Old South as much as rosewood parlor suites and Limoges china do wherever the magnolia and azalea bloom.

Loydia Linen Damask courtesy Brunschwig & Fils

© Dick Dietrich

Designing a Southern Room

OPPOSITE PAGE: *A finely detailed architectural frame-work and an underplayed color palette set off family heirlooms in Oak Alley, one of the South's most famous houses.*

ABOVE: *This classically elegant fabric belongs in a Southern home.*

61

Anyone who has recently glanced at the southern shelter magazines *Southern Living* and *Southern Interiors* can tell you that the elegance and hauteur that characterized the Old South have been reborn. From the Atlantic to the Mississippi, lovers of the glorious Southern past have successfully recreated interiors that even some Southerners suspect "are more sublime than anything we had in the old days." Consulting the glossy pages of these maga-zines, one can hardly believe that so many gorgeous objects exist. With their fond weakness for concen-trated opulence, America's Southern aristocrats are not unlike Spanish grandees.

Even though Southerners, like English nobles, have a history of polite rivalry and cultural compe-tition, they nonetheless adhered to exacting codes of behavior. The traditional Southern regional room is also bound by certain rules. With an emphasis on order, achieved using a prescribed vocabulary of Neoclassical elements that includes

ABOVE: *Neoclassical art objects and furniture are infinitely suitable elements of Southern style.*

TOP: *Because the rooms of row houses are often narrow, it is sometimes beneficial to remove unnecessary walls. The raised dining room adds interest to the progression of one room into another.*

columns, architraves, friezes, cornices, and the like, the "classic" Southern pillared mansion was a perfect expression of rule-bound antebellum society. These architectural directives are largely responsible for the resurgence of interest in classical Southern rooms. Because few modern interiors are built to the same strict rules of proportion, or indeed, with any detailing, classical or otherwise, some architectural adjustments must often be made to transform a modern space into a gracious Southern room. Fortunately, repetition and symmetry are a part of the formula for making a traditional Southern space. Thus, the tendency of modern developers to produce uniform interchangeable elements and spaces can be a plus. Irregular spaces, however, must be adapted to achieve this classical look. If, for instance, you have a room with just one window, placed in a corner, you could balance it with either a door or a false door or window. Don't laugh—even Thomas Jefferson resorted to such tricks as using false doors and windows in his Charlottesville home to create symmetry.

Oval and circular rooms are often found in gracious eighteenth-century houses. They are both difficult and expensive to build, but you can create an effective illusion of such a space in almost any room by installing an oculus, or circular opening, in the center of the room's ceiling and lighting it indirectly with tiny Christmas tree lights strung behind a molding. For a whimsical touch, try painting the recessed surface with a cloudy or starlit sky. Or, leave it white and apply Neoclassical ornaments made of plaster, fiberglass, or for an inexpensive adornment, wallpaper in relief. Below this oculus, place a round center table with a marble top. A pattern of concentric circles painted in faux marble on the floorboards or a round carpet would further support the illusion. To de-emphasize the corners of the room, focus on the curves. Place four columns, urns on pedestals, or statues in the corners. Or fill them with matching corner cupboards that can display a collection of family treasures.

The finely carved woodwork in classic Southern rooms was invariably painted white or a soft pastel. The furniture was generally produced in matching suites with a single color preeminent. These pieces were rather solid in outline, giving them a kind of sculptural stature that reinforced the architectural delineation of a room. Most often, continuous strips of patterned Brussels or deep-pile carpeting were fitted wall-to-wall. Because the rooms were so high-ceilinged and orderly, with matching furniture arranged all around the walls, the wallpaper and carpeting could be both strong and bold and the curtains both elaborate and theatrical. Some Southern furniture dating from the

LEFT: *Inspired by Charleston collections of Chinoiserie, this glazed chintz adds a Southern touch to any room.*

RIGHT: *This scarlet bedroom in Madewood in Napoleonville, Louisiana, has a majestic bed and crib. The group of prints is in perfect scale with the marble fireplace.*

© Dick Dietrich

63

Empire period (1815–1840) and the later Victorian era (the latter half of the nineteenth century) is so monumental in its magnificence of mahogany or rosewood that a single piece fills a modern room. Little else is needed. This is especially true in the case of the era's massive beds, some of which require stairs to be reached.

If you want to decorate a modern Southern room, there are two distinctly different propositions to consider. The first is a minimal approach, in which the end result will look as *Gone with the Wind*'s Tara might have appeared after the Civil War. With just a few gargantuan sculptural pieces of furniture in the Second Empire style, or perhaps in the florid Rococo Revival mode made famous by John Henry Belter of New York, you can eliminate most other elements. In a bedroom, for example, start with one of the impressive beds of the period, with a headboard almost as high as the ceiling. The bed linens should be all white, except perhaps for an old appliqué quilt. Drape the entire structure with gorgeous lengths of mosquito netting. You might even shroud the chandelier and possibly a picture in the stuff. You must also drape a chair, sofa, or chaise lounge with pretend dust sheets, perhaps in white-on-white damask. An old Victrola, dark mirrors, and an electric fan complete the set. For greenery, add a few palms and perhaps a potted gardenia. Wicker looks divine in such a fantasy atmosphere.

Of course, you could be more severe and modern and combine these same sorts of things made according to modern designs. The antithesis of this approach is the super-restored look I spoke of earlier in this chapter. It utilizes all the traditional elements of Brussels carpets, French gilded mirrors and porcelain, English silver, and matching suites of polished wood furniture. The difference, though, is that every conceivable kind of luxurious object is added to the room: jade lamps, tapestry cushions, fringes, and trimmings, for days on end. It's a complex and cluttered style, not really to everyone's taste, but when well done it can be quite intoxicating.

Chapter Three

THE WEST

PRECEDING PAGE: *Thick adobe walls, a raised corner fireplace, and beamed ceiling—all whitewashed—are a perfect foil for a tangerine colored floor in a room that readily recalls the old Southwest.*

RIGHT: *A square tile path shaded by a rough wooden pergola leads the way across the patio of this modern-day hacienda. The terra cotta oil jars are appropriate accessories.*

66

© Peter Paige

It's impossible to think of the American West without recalling the bold and dynamic images of the Wild West, as created by Hollywood. Some of the nation's best-loved movies have depicted the West as a rugged, larger-than-life land of great adventure that speaks to the individualist in all of us. If Eastern regional rooms are renowned for sophisticated elegance, Southern regional rooms for gracious charm and dignity, and country spaces everywhere for their relaxed comfort, what do Western regional rooms offer? All of the above is the correct answer. The basic thing to remember about the West is that almost everyone there passed through some other part of the country in order to "go West." The settlers of this region were more diverse in their backgrounds than those almost anywhere else. They also demonstrated a markedly laid-back outlook. The same pioneers who pragmatically abandoned grand pianos, furniture, and other nonessentials in order to get their well-loaded

An interior need not be a replica of an historic example to create Southwestern ambience. Here, a round, arched fireplace and plaster uplights evoke the West more fully than the decors found in many old rancheros.

© Peter Paige

67

wagons over the next pass nevertheless took values and ideas about what a house ought to look like with them.

Long treks over land or sea gave Western settlers a unique perspective on priorities, which gave them the ability to simplify their lives and homes. Although the settlers continued to cherish the architecture of and keepsakes from far-off homelands, Western regional rooms have a definitive clarity.

When you go west, the most striking thing about the houses you encounter between Texas and Washington is how well the best examples are wedded to the landscape. So much of the scenery, of course, verges on the overwhelming: the wind-swept plains and infinite horizon of Texas and the glorious beauty of the Southwestern desert, not to mention the inspiring Rocky Mountains and Sierra Nevada, the magical Redwood Forest, and the azure coastline. It all adds up to the great natural American majesty. Timid decoration just won't hold up in such surroundings. It is no surprise, then, that the mainstay of inspiration for regional rooms of the Old West has been the bold images of Native American art and the striking designs of the first European immigrants to the area—the Spanish. Neither could ever be mistaken as either tame or insipid.

© Peter Paige

The introduction of a glass wall behind this traditional Spanish-American fireplace successfully updates and lightens the style, which is usually solid and somber.

THE MARRIAGE OF SPANISH AND NATIVE AMERICAN STYLE

The decorative ideas of eighteenth-century Spain and Portugal were transformed by time and distance, as they were adapted to native conditions and available means. They were further blunted and simplified as they were introduced deeper into more remote areas, but the origins of Western style remain clear. Many visitors to Taos and Santa Fe just assume that the Southwestern look—expressed by adobe houses with beamed ceilings filled in with branches, floored with tiles, and heated by round-mouthed raised corner fireplaces—was derived directly from Pueblo traditions. Others, equally uninformed, attribute the look solely to the seventeenth-century conquistadors who came in search of gold. Yet this Western aesthetic was, like most American styles, a combination of Old and New World craftsmanship and design. Throughout the Spanish countryside—particularly on the coastal islands of Majorca and Ibiza—there are rus-

68

tic farmhouses every bit as primitive as those found in Arizona, New Mexico, and California. The islands' landscapes, in fact, look rather like the hill country of California. Interestingly, the adobe constructions of Native Americans resembled Spanish stucco. It was only logical that aspects of the New World familiar to the Spanish were whole-heartedly embraced.

Many people remain unaware of, or find it difficult to appreciate, the extent, duration, and accomplishment of Spanish colonization in North America. Yet before the establishment of the first English settlement along the Atlantic seaboard, the Spanish had already successfully explored the entire southern section of today's United States, from Florida to California. Their major focus was to conduct missionary activities, converting Native Americans to Catholicism. The Mission churches and cathedrals produced by this movement in the seventeenth and eighteenth centuries are some of the most ambitious architecture ever created in early America. They represent some of the most elaborate design and sophisticated engineering from this period. There was, for instance, a self-supporting masonry dome at the Church of San José y Sanmiguel de Aguayo at San Antonio almost one hundred years before the first dome of this type appeared in the Northeast. While there were iso-

© Balthazar Korab

69

lated instances when artisans were imported from abroad to execute the complex sculpture of the exuberantly baroque portals and altarpieces of churches, most often they were made entirely by Native artists. It was, in fact, partly the Native Americans' unfamiliarity with Spanish design and construction techniques that helped to simplify these buildings, concentrating most of the decoration in highly important portions of the structure. This principle also came to be applied in Spanish Colonial houses.

Santos and other antique wood carvings are given a prominent decorative role on the shelves and niches of a Spanish-American baroque fireplace. The Bokhara carpet and oriental screen add touches of color.

A striking, abstract painting offers an element of surprise in a traditional Southwestern dining room in which wood-framed leather chairs, delicate hand-blown glass, and graceful wrought-iron candelabrum harmonize with stuccoed walls, a beamed ceiling, and a terrazzo floor.

70

Dried-mud brick constructions covered in a smooth layer of clay—called adobe—had been used by the Native Americans for their communal, multi-story, set-back, flat-roofed houses for centuries. Spaniards adapted this method to European architecture. Although susceptible to erosion damage caused by infrequent rains, adobe's dry, porous nature provided excellent insulation from heat and cold. And it was cheap, with all the necessary components on hand. Native Americans used adobe in the most simple, straightforward way. Rough surfaces remained unadorned, corners were rounded, and buildings left irregular in layout. The resulting abstract, modern-looking structures have great appeal, which has attracted admirers from Frank Lloyd Wright to Georgia O'Keeffe.

The immediate impulse of seventeenth- and eighteenth-century European settlers was to control and dominate the natural environment. So even though the Spanish found the Native Americans' adobe houses ideally adapted to local conditions, they were quick to try to straighten and regularize the design whenever possible. The chaste and organic building style they first borrowed from the Native Americans soon gave way to increasingly fancier, more complex Spanish-American designs. Even in their earliest transitional buildings, rooms, windows, beams, and even porch columns were placed in neat, symmetrical order. However, the soft, rounded edges, raised corner fireplaces, beamed ceilings crisscrossed by branches covered with sod or clay, and tile roofs persisted.

The colors of Spanish American regional rooms are the earth tones of both desert and hill country. Almost invariably, the cream, buff, or ocher of adobe dominated monochrome interiors with contrast from dark, geometrically carved doors and shutters. Brick and tile floors were waxed to a dull sheen. Indian rugs and blankets were almost as prized as homemade or imported needlework-like flame-stitched cushion covers. All of these textiles provided welcome accents of color. Figures of saints, called *santos*, carved in wood and painted in natural colors, added more color accents that compelled the viewer to look at them.

Massive is the best one-word description of the painted and polished wood furniture of the ranchos and haciendas of the American West. North American examples are rare and the finest, most

A series of delightful and authentic regional features create a welcoming mix of the ornate and plain in this entrance hall. The adobe block walls and herringbone brick floor are painted, as is the intricate recess displaying a large Santos. The ceiling and border are painted in imitation of a scalloped canopy. Star-shaped lanterns are still made in the Southwest and in Mexico.

decorative pieces were made in Central and South America. Friar's chairs with pine, walnut, oak, and cypress frames and leather seats and backs studded with oversize nails were both imported or made locally. *Trasteros*, or food cabinets, made from evenly spaced, turned spool-like spindles, allowed ventilated storage and kept animals away from the food. *Armarios*, or clothes presses, took the place of closets and were often embellished with geometric paneling. Sometimes furniture and even walls were painted with gaily stylized floral motifs.

To augment seating space, since chairs were rare by today's standards, raised adobe platforms or benches for seating sometimes encircled rooms — just as in provincial Spain.

Native craftsmen, who had a long history of working with metal, became expert tinsmiths. Chandeliers with simplified baroque curves, sometimes coated in yellow varnish in imitation of gilt, cast a soft light about rooms and reflected off the whitewashed surfaces. Star- and sun-shaped lanterns of tin and glass produced an even more mystical glow in the cool shelters within thick adobe walls. Although sky blue and the purple and orange of a desert twilight sometimes found their way onto furniture walls or textiles in these rooms, more than anything else they formed the backdrops for Southwestern rooms.

© Balthazar Korab

71

FAR LEFT: *In keeping with the eclectic Spanish fashion of silent film era Hollywood, the Tiffany wisteria lamps, iron Gothic chandeliers, and enormous organ of the living room at Scotty's Castle in Death Valley evoke images of Rudy Valentino and Gloria Swanson dancing a passionate tango.*

LEFT: *Outfitted with rich and lustrous ornately carved woodwork, deep colors, tiled floors, and gilded stenciling, the 1870s Victorian Crocker Mansion in Sacramento, California captures the glory of gold-rush fortunes.*

73

VICTORIAN EXUBERANCE

Spanish Colonial Style

As soon as the railroads and manufacturers made Victorian goods and designs available out West, many of the ranchers and farmers there abandoned the old regional styles. Ultimately, the Sears and Montgomery-Ward catalogs that initially helped the inhabitants of the Western frontier feel connected to civilization even offered complete houses. As with European styles, Victorian eclectic architecture was late in reaching the West. But they made up for it in Galveston, San Francisco, and Eureka by building Victorian houses even more decorative and colorful than those back East.

A mirrored wall reflects a scene of contemporary Hollywood glamor made up of big leather chairs with gilded frames, oversized crystal goblets, an obelisk, and faux malachite-bordered china.

74

Club chairs (covered in crewelwork slipcovers) and abstract paintings are pleasant and unexpected additions to this Western fireside.

By 1900, Westerners began to reexamine their Indian and Spanish heritage. Architects trained in France at the Ecole des Beaux Arts created a stuccoed style called Mission. Adopting most of the elements of old Spanish American regional architecture, the Mission-style designers, not content to leave well enough alone, often added high-style Spanish Baroque and Italian Renaissance elements as "improvements." Some, like Irving Gill and Bernard Maybeck, added Japanese influences and an English Arts and Crafts sensibility to the Mission style to produce a look particularly associated with the San Francisco Bay area. Reacting against the fairy-tale exuberance of Julia Morgan's enchanted palace for William Randolph Hearst—the legendary San Simeon—designers like architect Paul R. Williams designed refined interpretations of Spanish Colonial houses for movie stars. The simplicity and elegance of his work was only surpassed by that of George Washington Smith at Santa Barbara and the brothers Green at Pasadena.

HOLLYWOOD REVIVAL

When the New York–based film pioneers abandoned their Astoria, Queens, studios for Hollywood's perpetual sunshine and shooting time in the 1910s, they brought their East Coast perceptions of glamour and elegance with them. Some of the Mid-Atlantic's most talented set designers, interior decorators, architects, and craftsmen also accompanied the moviemakers out West. Impressed by the possibilities of West Coast style, they nevertheless sought to temper its rugged, robust tendencies with East Coast notions of classical standards. The movie moguls, assuming a self-imposed responsibility to improve American taste, promoted this new Hollywood style.

Gradually, despite its origins as a super-refined version of the Spanish Colonial or Mediterranean

© Balthazar Korab

76

Despite the old-fashioned look of traditional open shelves and a 1930s vintage stove, this kitchen, decorated with quaint Santos and a jaunty Picasso print, is equipped with every modern convenience.

revival, the Hollywood style came to adopt stylistic props at random. These devices, whether a streamlined Colonial doorway or even paneling in the Louis XVI mode, were used as accents in well-proportioned spaces featuring classical symmetry. Because of the de-emphasis on ornament, whatever embellishment there was stood out in a sea of blank space like an exhibit in a museum. When combined with the geometric Art Deco ornament of the 1920s and '30s, with yards of sheer fabric, lustrous surfaces, and mirrors everywhere, this attractive style became a sensation copied around the world.

The grand moviemaking era of the 1920s and '30s introduced one of the most powerful and influential elements of Hollywood style—the great American swimming pool. Just as life in eighteenth- and nineteenth-century Spanish American houses centered around open-air patios or courtyards, so the life in modern Western houses revolves about the swimming pool. Surrounded by flowers and plants, furnished with painted wood or iron chairs

and lounges adorned with brilliant cotton cushions, shaded by enormous umbrellas, and often featuring a gas-fueled brick barbecue grill off to one side, the great outdoor space focused on the pool is the West's most recognizable regional room.

NORTHWESTERN STYLE

To the dismay of those who cherished its isolation, the American Northwest is becoming less and less remote. From the Cascade Mountains of Northern California to Portland, Oregon, to Seattle, Washington, the scenic wonders of national parks and a slow-paced way of life have attracted more new residents to the Northwest than ever before.

Ironically, most are seeking the increasingly elusive tranquility for which the area is world famous. Mysterious ocean currents help to moderate the climate along the ruggedly gracious coastline and provide abundant rainfall for still impressive stands of giant redwood, balsam fir, spruce, pine, and hemlock trees. A refuge for wildlife, the Northwest also attracts independent, proud people. There you will find the rustic architecture that was once common throughout secluded spots

© E. Alan McGee/FPG International

all over America. Cabins, lodges, and camps of the type once common in but now gone from the Catskills, Poconos, and Adirondacks are still abundant in the shadow of Mount St. Helens and Mount Rainier. Redwood is usually the building material out West, rather than the cedar logs frequently found in Eastern rustic houses. The carved and painted totem poles, baskets, canoes, and decorated paddles of Northwestern native tribes are integral elements of rooms in this region. Items such as wooden ceremonial drinking vessels, carved with spiritual figures in low relief with inlaid eyes of lustrous abalone, are prized today for their beauty and rarity.

Chairs and settees made from unstripped tree branches and twigs, cushioned with bright, homemade quilted pillows and bear and wolf hides, drawn near a boulder fireplace provided the perfect setting for a long winter night's relaxation before busy days once spent hunting and trapping but now often devoted to the ski slopes. One of today's innovations made practical by supplemental modern central heating are large windows that almost bring the outdoors inside. True Northwesterners are happiest when they are surrounded by the wilderness and can commune with nature. Kerosene lanterns, not the fancy ones, but the plain kind made of tin or glass with milky-white or dark-green

glass shades, are sometimes electrified today. Big, hospitable pine tables are also plain by design, and because nothing is ever wasted, they are sometimes surrounded by chairs made from old barrels. Wooden floors with wide boards are covered with sheepskins, Native American rugs, or the homemade, braided variety of old rag-rugs, and there's always a special one by the stove or fireplace—for the comfort of the family dog.

A chandelier made from an old wagon wheel casts a nostalgic glow over this log cabin's great room. Even though the stone fireplace and roughly hewn rafters fulfill the rustic Northwestern region's stylistic requirements, the comfortable chairs, thermal pane windows, and luxurious oriental rugs meet the overriding modern requirement that a room be lovely and inviting.

77

© Darryl Baird

© Balthazar Korab

79

Designing Western Rooms

The rough-hewn look of the Wild West has grown as popular in other parts of the United States as Mexican restaurants. A whole army of brick-face and stucco contractors now exist, ready to apply textured surfaces and rounded corners to your precise modern walls. Having achieved the structure of the West, what can you do to recreate a Western ambience at home? Well, for starters, unless you go after Hollywood style, the Western look tends to use a country mode of decoration. One of the most irresistible features of country decorating is that country furniture of all regional styles—and even some fancy furniture—fits happily together.

RIGHT: *In the kitchen of the house shown on the previous page, the same careful placement of windows and art objects employed in the living area is used to great advantage.*

FAR RIGHT: *Architects Bartos and Rose, and designers McMillen, Inc. used rose chintz, treillage-covered walls, potted palms, and a skylit ceiling to erase the line between outdoors and in.*

80

SPANISH COLONIAL – NATIVE AMERICAN ROOMS

Floors are probably the first consideration for easily introducing a Spanish Colonial touch. Although seldom seen outside of Spain, floors of pebble mosaic embedded in concrete create an authentic note. Straw or reed matting placed judiciously can make this sort of floor easier on your feet or can be used to entirely cover an ordinary floor. Tiles, whether the traditional quarry-tile squares or more colorful ones imported from Spain or Portugal, can be very dramatic. For an especially authentic and unusual impact you might even use such tiles in your living or dining room—apply either half-way or entirely up the wall.

If you aren't prepared to be this bold in your decorating, keep the walls plain as a backdrop for colorful Mexican glass pottery and textiles, which are inexpensive yet effective substitutes for antiques. Also attractive are modern versions of classic Native crafts: the famous black-on-black Navaho wedding jugs, colorful Native rugs, and the exquisite baskets of the Northwest Indians are all available as reproductions. Spanish-style reproductions can be found as well, including the sturdy carved Colonial-style benches, refectory tables, brightly painted ladder-back chairs with rush seats, and tin and glass star lanterns.

While it is important to remember to restrain color to achieve an authentic Western or Southwestern look, you can use color as an emphasis or focal point. Doors and backs of shelves or cupboards painted in a deep color can electrify an otherwise subdued decor. Produced in great quantities at the beginning of this century, Mission furniture in golden or gray-green "fumed oak" with leather upholstery is very practical as well as handsome. For a change from the predictable, though, use colored leather cushions that pick up the color of curtains or rugs.

Accents can include religious paintings and prints, which are usually slow sellers and underpriced, yet are perfect for Western regional rooms.

© Balthazar Korab

© Nancy Hill/FPG International

FAR LEFT: *A child's old bed loaded with pillows, walls banked by blooming plants, and skylights above log beams transform a one-time maid's room into an indoor patio.*

LEFT: *This superbly finished oak spiral staircase is proof that fine craftsmanship is still obtainable.*

Combine them with whimsically shaped mirrors or even groups of mirrors. White plaster urns and vases studded with bits of mirror are wonderful imports from India that look stunning in groups, as do classic Mexican ceramic vases in the form of stylized pineapples. Remember, however, that no matter what furniture or ornaments you employ in your Western room, be restrained. These rooms, more than most, need to achieve a feeling of space to be truly successful. So, even if you have a huge collection of monochrome American art pottery, either limit what you show to a small range of colors and shapes and rotate them (keeping most in storage), or show it all; but keep everything else in the room very low-key.

Low, built-in adobe benches directed toward a raised, hooded corner fireplace, sometimes highlighted by tiles, make excellent spaces to conceal air conditioning or heating ducts, plumbing, or just plain old storage. If your ceiling is low, paint it black or dark blue so that it floats above the whitewashed walls. Local nurseries or floral supply firms can provide you with flame-proof light beams that can be nailed in place over branches glued in a chevron pattern on the ceiling.

NORTHWESTERN STYLE

In ski areas such as Aspen, at resorts such as Lake Tahoe, and throughout Oregon and Washington, Western style is manifest in rustic lodges and cabins recalling the pioneer era. Log houses with enormous boulder fireplaces predominate in these regions. There are even a variety of mail-order prefabricated and custom cabin companies, from which you can order your own log cabin.

The Northwestern rustic home may be as simple as a one-room log cabin with a sleeping loft or as grand as a massive hunting lodge with fireplaces in each room. In each case, Northwestern flavor is provided by adding regional details. Native American crafts, including baskets, textiles, and carvings, add charm and authenticity. It is possible to engage Native craftspeople to sculpt totem pole–like columns for a porch or to support a living-room loft. Mementos from the days of trappers, prospectors, and pioneers, including old hand-held scales, family bibles, or tinware, bring the exciting frontier days alive in Northwestern regional rooms.

82

Reminiscent of the streamlined elegance of 1930s Hollywood, the geometric perfection of this room is juxtaposed with a picturesque landscape behind a wall of glass.

Lighting can be crucial to creating the proper atmosphere. Indirect lights angled down from amongst the ceiling beams and operated from a rheostat combine beautifully with heatless kerosene lamps outfitted with white or green glass shades to create the soft light appropriate to the Northwest. Wagon-wheel chandeliers and ceiling fixtures made from antlers are also evocative of pioneer days. (Don't despair if you like the look of antler furniture but hate the idea of hunting: Find out about companies that decorate furniture with antlers shed by male deer yearly.) Nothing looks better as an accessory in these hearty, basically masculine rooms than polished copper and brass. Use in light fixtures and other details. Old caldrons and kettles with plenty of dents and scratches make excellent planters or even bases for glass-topped coffee tables.

HOLLYWOOD STYLE

Hollywood glamour as a regional decorative style has been represented for decades in movies and television alike. Pale color schemes, lots of green plants, and oversize suites of upholstered furniture with innumerable oversize matching cushions typify the look. Dhuri rugs are the floor covering of choice in these interiors because of their flat weave, geometric patterns, and simple, muted colors. Antiques take a backseat in Hollywood regional rooms, where neither cost nor rarity are as important in furniture as style and dramatic presence.

Art Deco furniture, with its striking, rich, tropical hardwoods, gilded metal appliqués, marble tops, and stylized geometric designs, is perhaps the most desirable style for those who wish to create a glamorous setting. Its unique appeal lies in the combination of simplicity and luxury—a true Hollywood paradox. Sometimes designers combine

so many simple objects made of precious materials that the effect is as opulent as any Park Avenue penthouse. The main drawback to Hollywood style is that it is a formal look, requiring that all elements remain in place in order to keep the decor's structure from falling apart. It also requires frequent maintenance and replacement to keep fully up-to-date and sophisticated, for Hollywood style is always the latest style.

© Peter Paige

83

ABOVE LEFT: *Diagonal paths around the island counter are an alternative to a boxy room, as innovative and attractive as the pale pink ceiling.*

ABOVE: *Decorator Charles Damga demonstrates that a ceiling need not always be flat with a sky-painted barrel vault in this haut hip bedroom hung with old master reproductions.*

Chapter Four

© Alex McLean

THE MIDWEST

PRECEDING PAGE: *Many objects can reflect one's heritage or ethnic background. Here an African mask and a trio of early prints of Native American tribesmen recall the ancestry of historian Lanna Turner.*

RIGHT: *A Haitian painting, Indonesian animal carvings, rattan furniture, and a ceiling fan suggest a tropical environment.*

86

East or West, home's best—especially in the middle, many think. But just where is the middle of America, the beloved Midwest? Californians think of Ohio as "back East." New Yorkers are equally assured that Ohio is in the Midwest, and occasionally pronounce it "Iowa." Inhabitants of the region—from the Appalachians to the Mississippi, above the Mason-Dixon line—at least know where they are: in "God's own country."

Distinctive characteristics, or even a common history of the Midwest, might not be immediately apparent, yet there is a regional culture. Continuity of design principles, architecture, and decorative styles make the middle of the United States a fundamentally American place with its own regional identity. Its inhabitants, however, come from all over. Theirs is the legacy of independent-minded pioneers from New England, the Mid-Atlantic, and the South who headed inland to settle. The artistic vigor of these people was enriched by the contributions of Underground Railroad refugees from the 1700s to the time of the Civil War and the remnants of once-powerful Native American civilizations. The Midwest, with its vast spaces and endless opportunities, also accommodated several waves of immigrants to the United States. The result, in decorative terms, has been a mixture of distinctive ethnic styles amid certain common designs—a uniquely Midwestern style.

All of these inhabitants made the Western wilderness flourish into "the breadbasket of the world," as farms, big and small, extended over hill and dale and across the boundless plains. Indeed, for the first two hundred years of America's existence, as colonies and then as a nation, most citizens lived on farms. By the end of the 1870s, the transcontinental railroad had ensured the spread of Americans throughout the nation and encouraged the development of trade. Railroads helped create the golden days of farming in the region between

The historically correct elements of this room inspired by eighteenth century Scandinavia—painted furniture, sisal matting, and a bright floral mural—are freshly suited to today. The blue-and-white ticking Roman shades at the windows are both handsome and inexpensive.

87

Ohio and Kansas. The Civil War helped to further enrich Midwesterners, whose farms supplied the mighty Union army and occasionally outfitted Confederate troops as well. As America industrialized during the post–Civil War boom, the open spaces of the Midwest became dotted with factories and manufacturing plants as well. The wealth and opportunity represented by these farms and factories was like a magnet to people around the world.

By the end of the nineteenth century, immigration to America had reached an unprecedented level. While some newcomers stayed in the port cities where they first landed, most went inland to find jobs. Rubber, steel, glass, cars, coal, ore, grain, and corn were all produced in the Midwest. Immigrants in mighty waves swelled the cities, towns, and farms there, where more products were made better than anywhere else.

Aside from a powerful drive to succeed, most immigrants to America at some point in their history have shared an intense desire to fit into the American mosaic. Even if it meant discarding centuries-old traditions, for many immigrants the trade-off was acceptable. It is rather ironic today that the decorating craze for eighteenth-century Scandinavian, particularly Swedish, interiors, with bright textiles and painted, especially white, furniture, is virtually unknown in America's little Swe-

During the summer months the front porch is the most important "room" in any Midwestern house. The vines and stylish flower tubs decorating this Victorian example are especially appealing.

88

den at Minnesota. Similarly, African art, primarily sculptures of wood and bronze, was prized and collected by white Americans long before gaining appreciation among African-Americans. Except for an enduring legacy of ethnic humor, few of the movies produced in pre–World War II Hollywood indicate that the motion picture studios were founded mostly by Jewish Americans. Perhaps more than any other institution, the Hollywood of those days promoted "the American Way."

Nevertheless, many ethnic families worked hard to make their children aware of their heritage. Almost every household in America's various ethnic communities has preserved some bit of china, a wood carving, a religious shrine, or holy book, or other memento from the homeland. Linens worked by hand with traditional motifs were also daily reminders of where one's family had originated. Despite the appeal and value of such items, many newcomers felt a tremendous, not always subtle, pressure to turn away from their prized keepsakes and the places they symbolized. "It was almost a test of national loyalty," recalls a woman whose family landed at Ellis Island in 1910. Just this year a restored Ellis Island—the first place seen by many immigrants to America—reopened with great fanfare as a museum and genealogical center. This museum is probably the ultimate indication of how far we have come in recognizing the importance of the ethnic contribution to America. At last ethnicity is celebrated in a significant way, as an integral part of what it means to be American.

Perhaps no other kind of house brings to mind images of mom and apple pie as one with a big front porch. Whether on a huge old Victorian house located on the main drag of Duluth or a Kansas City bungalow, porches are all-American. When building a house in 1771, the American portrait

painter John Singleton Copley wrote a letter to his foreman stating his intention to build a piazza, as porches were then called. Piazzas were so new that Copley referred to his intended porch as a "peazer." When his contractor wrote back, "I don't comprehend what you mean by peazer," Copley responded:

> You say you don't know what I mean by a Peaza (*sic*). I will tell you then (*sic*). it (*sic*) is exactly such a thing as the cover over a pump in your Yard (*sic*)....3 or 4 Post (*sic*) added to support the front of the Roof (*sic*). A good floor at bottum (*sic*) and from post to post, a Chinese enclosure about three foot high... some have Collumns (*sic*) but very few.... These Peazas are so cool in Summer, and in Winter break off the storm so much that I think that I should not be able to like a house without [one].

Midwesterners from the late eighteenth-century to the present time have been wholeheartedly in agreement with Mr. Copley in this last observation. No house of any consequence in the region is without some kind of porch. Equipped with screens and thermal-pane storm windows, they have become the perfect compromise between living indoors and being outside. Attached to pool houses, or even standing free next to a barbecue grill, they make it possible to eat "outside" despite bugs, sun, or rain. Not seen too often today, striped canvas awnings helped dress up porches and windows in a festive way that announced the arrival of summer. They were also an efficient and nonpolluting method of cooling a house. The gala stripes that decorate canvas awnings were also often used to decorate the canvas-covered cushions on wicker, rattan, and wire porch furniture.

Many Midwesterners used their porches in the old days as outdoor living rooms all summer long. Swings, wooden or wicker, suspended from chains or in the form of sofa-like contraptions known as gliders, made for easy relaxation in those simple times. How many couples have courted over lemonade or iced tea while lolling on the porch in swings, gliders, rockers, and hammocks?

Period exterior color combinations documented in old paint catalogues offer great ideas for inside as well. The striped awnings of this late-nineteenth century house in Arkansas are a practical means to cool a room as well as being decorative.

89

90

Resplendent with white and purple lilac and a venerable chestnut tree, this house on Mackinac Island, Michigan boasts both a glass-enclosed sun porch and a sprawling front veranda.

Navaho rugs, jute matting, and even Oriental carpets helped contribute to the living-room air of front and especially side porches. As in the parlor, a matching suite of furniture was the rule for the "summer living room." Tea tables, rockers, chairs, chaise lounges—with handy magazine pockets and drink wells in the arms—and even lamps were made from wicker and rattan. Sometimes this furniture was left "natural." More often, however, in order to ward off the effects of weather, it was painted white, green, or black. Bird cages, fish tanks, a profusion of houseplants, and annuals like geraniums, begonias, and caladiums enlivened the porch. So, too, did portable phonographs inspire high spirits and informal dancing in the ancient,

pretelevision era, when time was spent on the great American porch.

In a way, it was Hollywood that created the great American suburb. Shaker Heights, Ohio; Indiana Village at Detroit; Oak Park, Illinois; or the ubiquitous Chestnut Hill—all those tidy Midwestern neighborhoods were both imitated and transformed by Hollywood's mythmakers. As a consequence, a house with a porch, a hall, a living room, dining room, den, kitchen, four bedrooms, and one or two bathrooms became an American icon. The parlors or living rooms of the houses typically had an ornamental fireplace flanked by built-in bookshelves, hardwood floors with oriental rugs, an upright or baby grand piano, and

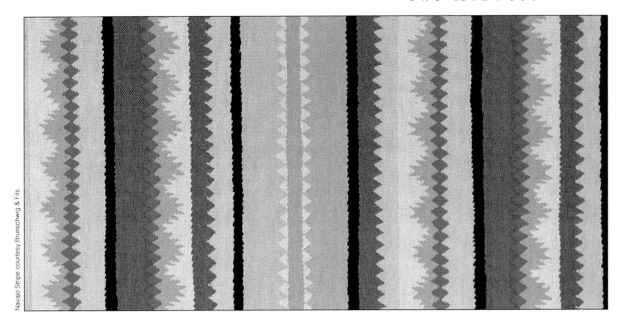

Navajo Stripe courtesy Brunschwig & Fils

matching catalog, or department-store furniture. Foreign commentators were impressed with the luxury of the establishments of middle-class Americans. However, more impressive, to ordinary Americans and foreigners alike, were Middle American bathrooms. Both the frequency with which they were encountered and the fact that, unlike European ones, they consistently worked, were a marvel for many people born before 1900. They were to witness the first general proliferation of bathrooms at the beginning of the present century. It's sometimes difficult to put ourselves in the place of our great-great grandparents, who were born at the end of the preindustrial bathroomless epoch. The brightest artificial illumination they knew during their youth was gas lighting. Today's shower and bathing functions were served by tin tubs brought out on the weekend. Wash and shaving stands in bedrooms had sets of china basins and pitchers for daily cleaning. A matching covered chamber pot stood ready under the bed to prevent nocturnal trips to the backyard outhouse or privy.

How life was changed by indoor plumbing and bathrooms! Many of the first ones were as big as bedrooms. Their unfamiliarity caused the uninitiated to wonder if they were altogether healthy. In 1854 one concerned man wrote his friend the following note:

Dear Jim:

I'm very much worried about you. I hear in Newport you are putting in two bathrooms. I never thought that you would be such a damn fool and expect to hear any day that you've been drowned.

James Moran

Folks less well off than Newport "swells" first installed bathrooms much later than the 1850s, of course. Their initial decorating instinct was often to treat the bathroom as if it were a scientific laboratory. Shimmering white square tiles covered floors and walls, ceilings were painted with white enamel as were mirror-fronted medicine cabinets and furniture. Fixtures—from the standard long tub on claw feet to the pedestal sink—were made of brilliant white porcelain on iron. Terry-cloth "Turkish" towels were also—you guessed it—white. This spartan look was completed by nickel- and silver-plated brass hardware that required incessant labor to stay sparkling. Even in the old days, the glacial quality of the all-white bathroom was sometimes off-putting. In order to make the new plumbing seem more acceptable to first-time bathroom owners, many manufacturers

ABOVE: *Restored, old-time fixtures like the marble and brass sink and claw-footed tub shown here can often cost less than characterless modern ones. The wall lights are reproductions. A nice detail is provided by the brass Victorian letter holder with clips in the shape of ladies' hands used to hold a guest towel.*

ABOVE LEFT: *This Navajo stripe might be found on a Midwestern porch.*

91

LEFT: *Originally stained and varnished, the wooden wainscotting of this twentieth-century bathroom has been painted green to harmonize with groupings of moisture-loving plants and a leaf of decorated wall-paper border.*

RIGHT: *A sophisticated black-and-white color scheme was used in designer Teri Seidman's renovation of this belle epoque bath where a Rococo border above the tiled wainscotting takes center stage. The porcelain cherubs above the pedestal sink and paintings of still more cherubs on the wall provide a romantic accent.*

decorated sinks, toilets, and tiles with ornaments in low relief in delicate glazed tints. Sea motifs such as shells, sea horses, and mermaids were commonly found in early bathrooms. Garlands of roses and other flowers were also big sellers. Sometimes the claw feet supporting tubs grasped glass spheres for an especially elegant touch. Hardwood enclosures that graced the very first zinc or copper stationary tubs, and toilets with overhead wall-mounted water tanks and pull chains gave early bathrooms visual warmth. These difficult-to-clean mahogany or walnut mountings soon came to be regarded as unsanitary, however. By the 1920s, in an attempt to restore to the bathroom something of this earlier "warmth," the Crane Company of Chicago and other manufacturers began to introduce color to the bathroom. Tiles were combined in contrasting colors and multiple shapes. The result, with colorful patterns on the floors and walls, often made the once-boring bathroom of the 1890s and early 1900s the most festive room in the house. By the middle of the decade, sinks, tubs, and toilets were also routinely made in color. Lime, pea, or emerald green, rose-pink, and lavender-violet were all popular bathroom colors. Fluffy bath mats and pretty translucent curtains that complemented the color arrangement were additions to 1930s bathrooms. So it was that the old hidden-away water closet emerged to show off heaps of style in the twentieth century.

92

Family photographs in silver frames and other keep-sakes are treasures that remind us of our roots.

94

ETHNIC STYLE

You may have been raised in an assimilated family without a single heirloom, but you'd still like to have your interior decor reflect the legacy of your ancestors. Where should you begin? First, try the great aunts, uncles, and other relatives. Even if your parents were not particularly interested in the family heritage, you never know what other relatives might have saved. Perhaps there are familial treasures that you've never seen. Don't assume that family keepsakes don't exist—they may simply be hidden away. Many relatives may be secret genealogy nuts who have been discouraged by their own generation's lack of appreciation for their passionate pursuit of family lore and mementos. Often you'll find that the younger generation has scant interest in these things. They may have inherited old

photographs, quilts, needlework pieces, icons, cedar chests, candlesticks, portraits, china, silver, and so on, which they have stored away. Some might be happy to pass them on to an appreciative collector.

Chinese Americans have long imported porcelains, silks, earthenware vessels, copper, and pewter. These wares are generally still made in China, although not always at the same quality level of older examples. In many urban Chinatowns these goods are available relatively cheaply. Rice pattern dinnerware can be a particularly handsome buy. Common elements like carp-shaped kites, paper fans, umbrellas, and lanterns can help transform ordinary interiors into subtly Oriental spaces. Rice-paper screens and window blinds are equally suggestive of China and Japan. Reproduction painted hand scrolls and folding screens are also imported from all countries in the Far East and very easy to find. Japanese wood-block prints depicting scenes

© Balthazar Korab

LEFT: *Stretching across the flat landscape, this elemental house with prominent chimneys evokes the prairie style aesthetic of Frank Lloyd Wright.*

BELOW LEFT: *The basic, unencumbered refinement of Japanese tea houses like this one built on an American estate at the turn of the century are perfectly adaptable to modern lifestyles.*

© Charles Fitch/FPG International

from everyday life, mythological subjects, and landscapes were highly influential with European and American Impressionist painters. The so-called Aesthetic Movement of the 1860s, 1870s, and 1880s freely borrowed Japanese motifs and elements for furniture, objects, and architecture alike. This explains why Japanese reproduction furniture, which looks so handsome and modern in monochrome, minimal contemporary settings, also stands up to the opulence of elaborate Midwestern, Victorian style environments. Full of rich color contrast, complex patterns, and varied textures, these rooms are complemented by the stark simplicity of Japanese furniture. The crane, a Japanese emblem of happiness, was perhaps the leitmotif of the Aesthetic Movement.

By encasing the sink in a granite-topped, wooden reproduction of an antique Japanese cabinet and subduing color to muted tones of gray, this humble powder room was transformed into a shrine to Shinto-inspired simplicity.

96

© Balthazar Korab

At the end of the last century, German-American communities often contained homes with regional rooms that almost literally adapted the grandeur of baronial great halls with dark oak furniture, collections of beer steins, and rows of antlers. Many of these Germanic elements, including massive, heavily carved furniture; tapestries; and salt-glazed blue and cream-colored stoneware, are, after decades of disfavor, finding their way into antique shops and from there into new German-American rooms. While there is no such thing as Jewish-American furniture or interior decoration, this German look closely approximates the cozy interiors that many Jewish immigrants recreated in New York's Washington Heights and other German-Jewish-American enclaves, beginning in the mid-nineteenth century. In addition to the displays of Rococo Revival Dresden figures, or highly ornamental white wine Hock glasses with cut and colored tulip-shaped bowls atop a tall stem, these German-Jewish-American interiors often contained Judaica. Many people still have substantial heirloom dining tables with extra extension leaves and Belgian lace or linen damask tablecloths to cover them. Here were held those memorable family feasts, traditional meals of rice pudding, borscht, chicken soup, pot roast, and Halvah that were eaten amid joyful family exchanges framed by the beauty

of religious ritual. The Sabbath candlesticks and the Menorah, the latter reserved for the week-long winter festival of lights called Hanukkah, were often handmade from silver. These heirlooms were usually embellished with ornaments of symbolic significance. The Star of David, the Lion of Judah, the tablets of Moses' law—these emblems have recurred throughout the centuries. They constitute the sacred vocabulary of Jewish religious text and implements, which grow increasingly collectible and valuable.

African-American memorabilia, even advertising-art for products like Aunt Jemima's Pancake Mix or Gold Dust Twin Soap Powder, though ste-

reotypical and sometimes overly satirical, are very collectible. Positive Black images, though rare, are possible to find, often as illustrations accompanying nineteenth-century articles in journals like *Harper's Weekly*. If you don't relish the idea of cutting up these period magazines, photographic reproductions or photocopied prints can be made on good quality paper, hand-tinted, and framed. Although quilts made by Southern Black grandmothers are quite rare as a result of the small number originally made and hard everyday use, expert African-American quilters, especially in tourist towns, will happily oblige your desire for modern versions of this useful, beautiful artwork.

An enormous table able to accomodate every member of the family was once found in every Jewish-American household. The Tiffany window depicts Penelope spinning as she awaits the return of Odysseus.

In a Harlem brownstone, interior designer Timothy Van Dam reintroduced an Aesthetic Movement color scheme with blue walls and an Indian red cove as a setting for the owner's collection of African artifacts. The Middle Eastern brass lantern was found in an area thrift shop.

© Alex McLean

In urban centers, the photographs, literary first editions, prints, sculpture, paintings, drawings, posters, and playbills produced by Black artists during the so-called Harlem Renaissance of the 1920s are competitively sought. As a result, prices for the works of painters Henry O. Tanner and Jacob Lawrence, the sculptor Richmond Barthe, and the photographer James Van Derzee have shot through the roof. Although few collectors can afford pieces by these very popular artists, much of the work of lesser-known contemporary Black artists remains overlooked in obscure neglect. This work is very collectible. "Check out who the local Black artists were in the 1920s, 30s, 40s and 50s. Local historical societies probably have back issues of African-American newspapers and magazines from the period that identify them," advises the African-American architect John Reddick. "Their work, often unrecognized today, can be found for

very little, although it does take hunting." Finally, he reminds the prospective Afro-centric collector, "Don't forget to encourage living African and African-American artists. They hold the legacy of our history and contributions in trust for the future."

Antique African art, although increasing in value, is still obtainable. Be forewarned, though, as with all ethnic artwork and crafts that are still manufactured in the authentic manner of genuine antiques, unscrupulous dealers sell facsimiles as the "real thing." Protect yourself by learning as much as you can about the objects you buy and whomever you buy from. This said, as usual, remember that reproductions have real decorative value in regional rooms. Not only are they affordable, but they're decorative as well. Modern masks are a good example. Mass-produced for tourist and foreign markets, the masks permit you to embellish

An early eighteenth-century Dutch marquetry cabinet is a fitting repository for a collection of seashells, Chinese roosters, and a Portuguese vase in the shape of a Blackmoor's head with Indian corn plums emerging from his turban.

© Alex McLean

or alter them without fear of destroying great art. As a rule, it is considered almost immoral to deface an artist's creation, even if it is humble. However, stripping or painting a collection of inexpensive wood carvings can give them a dramatic impact that improves their decorative value. I've seen quite ordinary reproduction Yoruba and Ibo masks painted flat black then decorated in white with designs imitating traditional tribal face painting. When the masks were displayed against a coral-colored background, the effect was stunning. It would have been equally dramatic to use white masks on a black background. Track lighting further enhances such groupings.

© Alex McLean

100

***Early photographs and prints depicting Americans
with ethnic ancestry can still be found.***

This dramatic effect needn't be limited to
African masks. San Francisco's Chinatown and
Japantown, German Village in Columbus, and
Santa Fe's Old Town—indeed, most American
ethnic communities—are excellent sources for inexpensive raw material for creating ethnic regional
rooms. Because these items are so common and
cheap, sometimes there is a snobbish tendency to
overlook the possibilities they offer. However, no
less an authority than Tom Britt, who has probably
designed more *Architectural Digest* cover rooms

than anyone else, urges the use of such elements to
make a bold statement. "It's all a stage set, honey,
in the end," he reassured a client recently who
expressed doubts about four gigantic Japanese
lanterns that the persuasive Mr. Britt urged using
to define the borders of a cube-shaped entrance.
"The house is along the Northern California coast,"
he explains. "It's very refined, with symmetrical
stripped down Neoclassical architecture not unlike
that of the eighteenth-century English designer Sir
William Taylor. We wanted to keep everything

© Richard Mandelkorn

quite simple and elegant. We used the same color throughout, a kind of apricot. Although the furniture consists of mostly white raw silk, upholstered Bill Baldwin slipper chairs, a few big divans, and a huge ottoman in the center, we used oriental antiques as accents. The look overall," Britt stresses, "has the same severity and open light qualities as traditional Japanese houses." The Western touch is his usual formal symmetry instead of the typical asymmetry of Japanese spaces. "The subtle tension of East meeting West this way makes a dynamic statement" he said.

A big part of Britt's plea for creativity would seem to urge disregard for stylistic purity. In the same California house he mixed old and new, classical and modern, Eastern and Western elements with aplomb. How can different ethnic styles be mixed? One suggestion is to use just one wall, floor, and upholstery color to make a uniform, uninterrupted background. In this way, spaces can flow into each other. Whatever added focal incidents of unique color, pattern, or decorative accents you use won't clash in such an environment, so long as you limit their number or employ objects of related colors, shape, and, type. Put most simply: simple, plain objects look good against an elaborate or complex background, just as ornate, monumental

objects stand out against and add needed interest to a restrained background. If you have plain floors and walls and lots of space, you can make the room smaller and more intimate by contrasting the color from one room to another. Entering into a low, dark rotunda from the sunny outdoors, you'll get a heightened impact coming into an adjoining higher, larger, lighter room. To keep this contrast from seeming too abrupt, use upholstery, curtains, or rugs that either pick up or repeat the color and motifs in the next space. Whatever your inspiration for your Midwestern or other regional rooms, take the time to explore the possibilities of having what you want. "Don't be afraid to try things out before you make a final decision," instructs "the Professor," esteemed decorative-arts historian Stanley Barrows. "Rose Cummings, one of America's great ladies of interior design, always moved things about over and over. She knew just what she wanted— once she saw it." So, as they say in the Midwest, "Follow yer instincts."

So long as the minimalist essential principles of the Shinto-Buddhist tradition are kept in mind, it is possible to duplicate Japanese style with modern Western elements. The positioning and lighting of the focal artwork are especially effective.

Chapter Five

COUNTRY STYLE

PRECEDING PAGE: *Pale cotton printed fabric from India was used to form a graceful canopy over a child's pine bed and to drape an easy chair in a pretty country guest room.*

RIGHT: *The punkah or ceiling fan in this rural bed chamber denotes Southern climes. Otherwise, the honesty of whitewashed walls and beautifully crafted homemade textiles are traditional aspects of country decor throughout the nation.*

104

All over America, people enthusiastically refer to their preference for "country"—country houses, country life, and country style. To different folks, though, these terms can convey an almost bewildering variety of meaning. Lots of people think of life in the country as not so very different from their city existence. Transported to more or less rural settings, their country "cottages" come replete with facsimile machines and computers mixed in among fine French antique furniture. Other country lovers find fulfillment in a sort of glorified camping lifestyle, with only the crickets to serenade them at sundown and the closest newspaper, telephone, or cup of cappuccino, miles away. Somewhere in between these two extremes are the country experiences enjoyed by most Americans.

The differing interpretations of country have everything to do with regional custom and, not surprisingly, are best observed in regional rooms. City influenced, highly structured country houses are more likely to be encountered outside bustling urban centers like New York, Dallas, and Chicago.

By long-standing reputation, the West Coast is inclined to be more casual. Country places there are often laid back, with the local social life centered around hot tubs and swimming pools. (Of course, the traditional Hollywood influence in Southern California once imbued even the simplest spaces with style and glamour.) The West Coast is renowned for its fashionable trendsetters, among them no less an arbiter of taste than *Architectural Digest* editor in chief Paige Rense, who is helping to bring about the demise of over-elaborate decora-

Featuring low ceilings, carefully made stone walls, and naturally finished woodwork, country houses by modern master Frank Lloyd Wright perpetuated a vibrant legacy from the past.

© Mark E. Gibson

tion—at least in the country. Through the example of her own sequestered retreat, chock-full of rustic, down-home antiques and folk art, she has helped to promote a look more in tune with the area's placid state of mind.

Up north, though, Southern Californians will tell you, especially around the San Francisco Bay area, people are more reserved, households more dignified, and regional rooms in the country more like those in the city.

Several options lie between these extremes. Particularly along the southeastern coast of the United States, relaxed country charm and elegant country formality have been successfully combined. As one matron of the old school says, "Decorum is a central element of Southern country life. Whether they're reared in a white-pillared mansion or a log cabin, Southerners can eat fried chicken with their fingers and still remain dignified."

Despite the range of distinctive regional manifestations of country style, there is one thing country rooms all share: the rural setting where they are found. Thus, it is rural history that gives American country style its traditions.

Country furniture reveals a history that parallels the evolution of farmhouses and other rural architecture. In each case country folks started with the basic necessities, then gradually exchanged the

The crude log walls of this country cabin were roughly axed by tools like those displayed on the gingham-covered table. Old handmade wooden bowls are increasingly collectible.

familiar for the fashionable. Sometimes this process occurred slowly—often, cautious farmers took so long in adopting a new style that it grew old-fashioned in the process. Greek Revival architecture and the corresponding Empire furniture are a good case in point. As Neoclassicism became fashionable both here and abroad, they initially appeared in cities along the Atlantic, from Boston to Savannah, in about 1810. In the Eastern countryside they failed to have a major impact until around 1825. Later still—circa 1830—Neoclassical elements made their first appearance west of the Alleghenies.

The fidelity with which pioneers recreated the architecture and furniture they remembered of home could be quite remarkable. Differences basically resulted from the five to ten years it took for the Eastern styles to reach the frontier. Pattern books were one source of designs, although furniture makers relied less heavily on them than architects did. Consequently, furniture styles tended to be more current. After all, a cabinetmaker could fairly easily copy a new high-style chair or table imported from Boston. Local builders occasionally sent away for building designs in the latest taste.

Spirited and dynamic, the mustard yellow and black color scheme, stylized chandelier, and Venetian blinds of this early American room might not seem to be authentic to those who associate soft pastels and elaborate decoration with the epoch—but they are.

As country folk so often said of architectural styles and everything else, "If it ain't broke, why fix it?"

This was also very much the attitude of Pennsylvania's early German settlers at York and Egypt. Both towns retain dwellings very similar to farmsteads once found in the Black Forest region. These mid-eighteenth-century structures contain steeply gabled tile roofs, with flaring eaves and shed dormers. Some even have half-timbered walls filled in with brick. All these features speak of the old country. What remains a controversial subject, though, is the origin of the area's log houses. These Eastern structures were clearly the prototypes for the West's legendary log cabins, but where did they originate? Many cite Switzerland or Scandinavia, others insist that the Native Americans were the first to erect log buildings.

In any event, European styles and city fads were usually transformed in replication in the countryside or wilderness. This was because of the tendency to simplify when interpreting a new style, as well as the need to make adjustments or incorporate new elements to suit the specific environment. Not unlike the Connecticut valley farmers before them who felt a new-style front door, stairway, or mantlepiece adequate to express their enlightened modernity, pioneers in the West were also often content with symbolic up-to-dateness. Transitional buildings and furniture in the country therefore frequently contain a startling juxtaposition of old and new features. It is for this very reason that these hybridized designs can be refreshingly imaginative.

Moreover, in regional rooms of the country, the humbler materials, less exacting craftsmanship, and sense of fun with which furniture was made produced a more relaxed atmosphere. This quality is the antithesis of that polished perfection characteristic of high-style period rooms like those on exhibit in the American Wing of New York's Metropolitan Museum of Art. In the country successful decors were not so much made as born. They were developed in the same kind of organic process that formed country houses historically. Rooms, ells,

OPPOSITE PAGE: *Although they are greatly simplified and often reduced in scale, the decorations and designs of classic eighteenth-century French country furniture were identical to their city counterparts. Simplification of country pieces included the replacement of vivid cotton prints with delicate silk upholstery. The contrasting gingham back is indicative of the eighteenth-century custom of putting chairs around the room with their backs against the walls.*

LEFT: *Quilted patterns are quintessentially country.*

BELOW: *The powerful presence of these modern quilts made in Pennsylvania is compelling.*

and lean-tos were all added as required. In the course of a lifetime, needs changed and country rooms, which didn't rely on the meticulous coordination of matching elements, were eminently accommodating. They still are today—which is why stenciled chambers with checked curtains, log-cabin quilts, and Windsor chairs, and beamed halls with limestone floors, waxed walnut panels, and painted Louis XV furniture are both called country rooms by their inhabitants and equally loved.

COUNTRY
VARIATIONS

The Amish and Shaker Styles

Universally, one of the most important lessons of history is the old adage, The more things change, the more they stay the same. Incredible though it may seem, this saying applies especially to the American regional room and the history of its decorative treatment. People's views and values—what they believe in and admire—have always had a profound impact on the spaces they inhabit. In

the past, as today, countless religious groups, political factions, and other movements have sought freedom to express their beliefs and found it in this country. Even in America, many have had to struggle in order to pursue a course outside of the mainstream. Nonetheless, the pursuit of liberty is what distinguishes this remarkable nation.

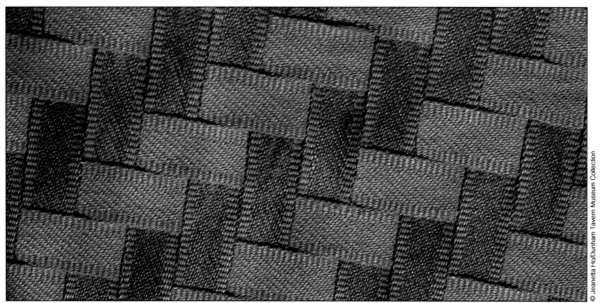

ABOVE: *A sample of the woven seat on a Shaker chair from the Dunham Tavern Museum in Cleveland, Ohio.*

RIGHT: *The subtle variations of geometry and strong and precise symmetry of Shaker furniture and architectural design recall the deceptive simplicity of a Mozart symphony. The ladder-back chairs were kept out of the way on pegs around the room until needed.*

110

From a decorative standpoint, two of the most influential religious bodies in America were the Amish and the Shakers. The Amish are a strict Mennonite sect that originally settled in Canada, Pennsylvania, Ohio, and Indiana, descendants of the seventeenth-century Swiss bishop Jakob Amman. The Shakers were an English Millenarian group who believed in lifelong celibacy and the common ownership of property. Although they had little else in common, both groups eschewed direct involvement in what they perceived as the debased and worldly existence of humankind. This withdrawal from vanity fair was manifested in their crafts in a refined aesthetic that rejected all extraneous embellishment. In fact, any elements deemed superfluous to function were generally discarded. The most famous results, Amish quilts and Shaker furniture, are distinctly American triumphs of design. Celebrated as works of art throughout the world today, these objects from the past astonish us with their elemental utility and beauty. To our eyes they have a farsighted modernity.

Despite the restrictive discipline of these spiritually motivated aesthetics—or perhaps because of it—Amish quilts and Shaker furniture reveal the fertile imaginations of their creators. Both show a great variety of form and design, albeit along common themes. There is a beauty emanating from

112

New quilts, incorporating old, sometimes symbolic patterns, are still made in many regions today. These future heirlooms are as comforting to the soul as to the body.

simple Shaker furniture that can almost be described as joyous. From today's perspective it may be difficult to understand how people who had rejected the indulgent temptations of the world and practiced celibacy could have created such sensual objects. However, from its founding, Shaker theology embraced the expression of joy throughout one's life as a basic tenet of faith. Originating in England in 1741, the Shakers were named after the frenetic dancing that was a part of their religious observances. They advocated communal living, although with men and women in separate houses. By the mid-nineteenth century there were Shaker colonies all over the Eastern and Midwestern United States. They were well known for their superb farms. Indeed, their skills as plant hybridists and livestock breeders were as legendary in the past as their furniture is now.

Shaker furniture is characterized by fine materials, fashioned by hand into objects with near-perfect, machinelike, geometric precision! A good deal of their furniture was built-in, particularly cupboards, wardrobes, and chests of drawers.

Clothing was hung from Shaker cloak pins that were built into bedroom paneling. With great elegance, Shaker craftsmen transformed the ordinary furniture types of their time into paeans to simplicity. Hepplewhite tripod candlestands with three curving legs connected to a central stem were distilled to form a graceful play of lines. Conventional four-poster beds with lathe-turned, urn-shaped posts were translated into stark yet exquisite forms with highly attenuated, tapered posts of toothpick slenderness. Native ash, curly grained maple, birds-eye grained birch, walnut, and cherry were used instead of popular tropical hardwoods such as mahogany and satinwood. Pine, poplar, and other soft woods, known as whitewood, were invariably covered in clear shades of paint.

Like so many of the world's great artistic achievements, Shaker furniture has such a straightforward appearance that one might believe that it was easily made. Such assumptions are belied by the fact that even the finest of modern replicas are somehow lacking in comparison to authentic Shaker pieces. Maintaining their numbers solely by

conversion and through the adoption of orphans, the Shakers achieved a peak membership of about six thousand around the time of the Civil War. Currently their numbers are approaching a scant half-dozen souls. This is the same number that had originally accompanied Mother Ann Lee to New York in 1774 to establish the Shakers in America.

The many German immigrants who first came to the United States seeking religious freedom and good fortune, including Baptists, Seventh Day Adventists, Harmonists, and many more, were all the fruit of Martin Luther's quest for a reformed, more direct expression of faith. All were received with open arms by the Quaker statesman, William Penn, who truly practiced the brotherly love he preached. Pennsylvania thus welcomed settlers of all persuasions, in sharp contrast to more restrictive colonies such as Massachusetts, where none but Puritans were tolerated at first.

Amish quilts reverberate with the same joyful expression seen in Shaker furniture. Named for the Swiss Bishop Jakob Amman who broke with the Mennonite church in the late seventeenth-century, many Amish still live in the idyllic farm country of southeastern Pennsylvania. Like Mennonites, the Amish are opposed to political involvement, holding public office, oath taking, or military service. They also disdain the modern world's omnipresent

gadgetry—from cars to computers. Their quilts are singular celebrations of devotion, though this might not be readily apparent to outsiders. Rejecting worldly printed fabrics, Amish needlewomen use only solid-colored materials. Yet perhaps to compensate, they often employ exquisitely stitched quilting in astonishingly intricate patterns. The relationship of contrasting pieces of fabric in these works is deceptively simple. Their uncontrived repetitions of stripes, known by the biblically inspired names of Rainbow or Jacob's Coat can be as stunning as any of Frank Stella's wonderful paintings of bands of saturated color.

Aside from the nostalgia for a less complicated time that they inspire, Amish crafts owe their appeal also to their seemingly magical transformation of little or nothing in the way of materials into precious works of art. Although exquisite, these crafts are also uncomplicated, approachable, and inviting.

A classic Amish quilt is so straightforward by way of design that one might fail to notice its exquisite craftsmanship at first glance.

© Phillip H. Ennis

114

Derived from high style prints of the seventeenth-century Old Master floral patterns, this typical Pennsylvania Dutch motif is a sprightly emblem of abundance. The grained frame is original to this early nineteenth-century work.

PENNSYLVANIA DUTCH STYLE

Despite old trusted methods of building, like half-timbering filled in with brick, numerous easily quarried ledges of limestone have caused stone houses to become synonymous with Pennsylvania. The porous masonry was easy to work but difficult to dress, so it usually appeared as stones roughly laid with thick, white-lime mortar.

In eastern Pennsylvania's Amish country or among the unspoiled storybook hamlets of the Brandywine valley, imposing frame barns on stone foundations also dot the verdant landscape. Painted a robust red, they are emblazoned with good-luck motifs called hex signs. Each had its specific meaning: health, prosperity, protection from evil, and so forth. These emblems were painted on furniture as well. Official papers, including deeds and marriage and birth certificates were also inscribed with these ancient designs in the 1700s and early 1800s. Marriage or dowry chests, which were made to contain trousseau linens, were singled out for traditional designs remembered from the immigrants' European past. Rampant prancing unicorns, for example, symbolic of purity, joined brightly painted stylized flowers to create an overall pattern. Most such decorations were dated; the earliest remaining are three hundred years old. Some also bore the name of their original owners.

The rooms in which these chests stood were sparsely furnished with trestle tables and plank chairs with fancifully shaped backs modeled after Tyrolean originals. The chairs were sometimes carved with stag heads in bas relief, but the vibrant chests were still the primary focus in the room.

Pennsylvania attracted more continental European immigrants than any other of the original

The charming sprigged paper in this kitchen picks up the floral decoration of the old stencilled chairs. Because of sympathetic coloring and floral designs, the Majolica ware plates fit right in.

115

© Phillip H. Ennis

thirteen colonies. Many among them were highly accomplished craftsmen. William Henry Stiegel, for instance, is considered to be the father of American glass. A good deal of his precious glassware was enameled in bright colors with the same folk designs found on Pennsylvania Dutch chests and illuminations. A type of glass once made in shops like that of Stiegel, which is still produced in New Jersey, is the so-called South Jersey glass, first made in the mid-1700s. Distinguished by gathers of glass called lilypads, it was made in several colors into vessels both useful and decorative. Older examples with tiny bubbles, ripples, and other imperfections have a highly fluid look.

English in derivation, the Windsor chair was another specialty of Pennsylvania craftsmen. Eliminating the pierced splat found in the backs of the original examples, the craftsmen produced a more graceful design. This feature was actually left over from the Queen Anne era, when it was grafted onto vernacular turned William-and-Mary style chairs. American scooped saddle seats were also deeper, so the chair became more comfortable. A preoccupation with comfort of body, mind, and soul is at the very essence of the warm and friendly style of Pennsylvanian rooms graced by Windsor chairs. The enduring foundation has guaranteed this style's longevity and continuing popularity.

Designing a Country Room

Whether formal or rustic, in town or in the wilderness, believable country rooms have a fundamental element in common: flowers. Nothing else so perfectly imbues an environment with basic country charm. Fresh flowers may be found all year long at florist shops and in your own yard during warmer months. For city-dwellers, trips to the countryside are a wonderful opportunity to bring back flowers. The effort is worth it; you will be rejuvenated and refreshed by your flowers. Nurseries, roadside farmers' stands, fields, and parks are all excellent sources for old-fashioned blooms and wildflowers that are usually unobtainable in the city. These country sources are usually quite dependable, but of course there is an even better means of assuring an affordable profusion of blooms.

"A garden," said Alexander Hamilton to a colleague, "is, as you know, the usual refuge for a disappointed politician." Therapeutic benefits aside, a garden also offers an extremely convenient source of flowers and even vegetables. A friend's or relative's garden may substitute if you have no space for

LEFT: *By eliminating color, designer Marietta Gomez has created a fresh environment in which antique stripped pine, 1950s rattan, and a quixotic wind vane enhance the open flowing comfort of a great room in the country. Every element was purposely chosen for its simplicity, yet subtle touches of elegance abound. Note for instance, the blue strip woven into the sea grass floor mat, which is repeated in the striped ticking covering the sofa.*

ABOVE: *A pretty floral chintz is a perfect choice for a country room.*

117

According to landscape designer Kevin Wolfe, "No other undertaking is as suggestive of country pleasures as a garden laden with flowers, fruits, and vegetables, which derive superior freshness, aroma, and flavor from being homegrown."

118

a garden. Your own Eden, however, even if it is only a weekend enterprise, can be endlessly satisfying. If you've never lived in the country or cultivated a small plot in your backyard, you might not at first appreciate the romance of gardening. You might even be skeptical about the superior experience of eating corn or tomatoes straight from your own garden versus those purchased from the city grocer. The difference between dry, commercially packaged herbs and the homegrown variety might also

seem insignificant—until you try them. Upon your first taste of country produce you will know the pleasure of heretofore unimagined taste sensations. For many people the difference between fresh and packaged produce is so profound that they take the trouble to garden in the city. On rooftops and terraces, in courtyards, and window boxes, fresh vegetable and flower lovers have made oases in the concrete. These spots are all the more attractive because they are unexpected.

Chock full of nineteenth-century dog portraits, flowers, and candles, Mario Buatta's signature look is rooted in the country-life tradition, notwithstanding its polished elan.

In a Greek Revival farmhouse in Bath, Ohio, interior decorator Terry McCuan transformed a sideporch into an all-year indoor garden room. Skylights that can be opened in summer augment the original French doors. The ceiling fan circulates rising heat in winter and vents hot air in summer. Emulating seventeenth- and eighteenth-century colonial style, the Oriental carpet is used to cover the table rather than the cream-colored tile floor.

It is partly this element of surprise that has helped to popularize many American regional room styles. In a big-city apartment, certainly no room is so delightfully unanticipated as one that recalls rural places. If you have large windows with favorable light you can transform an ordinary room into a sort of country winter garden or conservatory. Simply paint the floors and find quilt tops to use as tablecloths. The type of plants you select can refine your regional room theme. Potted primroses, African violets, ivy, geraniums, and ferns, suggest Eastern country rooms, evoking New England, Pennsylvania Dutch, and Shaker style. Cacti, palms, and succulents lend a Southwestern or Western flavor. For a Californian or Northwestern country note, try bonsais, azaleas, gardenias, or Norfolk pines planted in wooden tubs or large ceramic or terra-cotta containers. Skylights and ceiling fans contribute both comfort and a bright airiness to country-style rooms.

It is not only fresh flowers that capture the cheerful quality characteristic of the country room; dried flowers have long been associated with country as well. The most common country motif, found on wallpaper, fabric, rugs, paintings, and other surfaces, is flowers, although plants, vegetables, animals, and other natural images are also suggestive of a pastoral lifestyle.

A seminal collection of hand-crafted objects—wooden decoys, a salt-glazed pitcher, and a tinware candle-stick—forms an ideal tablescape in a country room.

121

All too often, the furniture you already have is too ornate or, conversely, too modern, to use as-is in your country decor. Many pieces may be too valuable to paint or re-cover and others, while useful, may be of too little value to be worth the time and effort. Fabric can be key in this regard. Slipcovers and table skirts can conceal a multitude of deficiencies, while adding a colorful touch. Although multicolored chintzes remain perennial favorites for country places, some designers are growing a little tired of what they term the English disease. These decorators have begun to revive the idea promoted by late decorating giant Billy Baldwin of covering everything in white duck cloth or linen. This scheme evokes a scene of perpetual summer— which is the essence of country. It had its origins in vacation villas and seaside cottages furnished with wicker and hung with ruffled organdy curtains. An alternative for chintz lovers who nonetheless would like to update their country look is chintz or blocked linen with a dark background. The famous French version of this printed linen fabric has a white background and is called *toile de Jouy*. It is printed from engraved copper plates that often depict historical scenes. Another effective look is achieved by combining fiber matting on the floor with subdued wall color and the use of toile fabric on all the furniture and for curtains as well—

this scheme produces a surefire country freshness. If you aren't going to have white on white, or white and one color, or color with white accents, then avoid white altogether. As Ron Wagner, a popular New York interior designer, often cautions clients, "Nothing is more difficult to make interesting and vital than a white or beige room. Wallpapers and stencils are de rigueur country."

To furnish regional rooms entirely with authentic objects is likely to be both prohibitively costly and very time-consuming. However, consistency is crucial: always use the very best you can afford, and be sure to transform or disguise any inferior elements. It is an art to mix plain and fancy, the ordinary and the extraordinary. In a room where you've pared most everything to a low-key level—as if to form a background—you would ideally show off a few "stars," or outstanding pieces. A country room might have large modern sofas covered in Schumacher's fabric woven in patterns modeled on the red, white, and blue handwoven Ingram coverlets made in the United States from circa 1820 to 1870. Combined with reproduction Shaker furniture or perhaps some Hitchcock chairs, the room would come to life with the addition of an authentic antique or heirloom star. On the other hand, if you wanted to make a large collection of spongeware or yellowware country ves-

Old prints like this Currier and Ives view of a long-ago sleigh race are inexpensive decorations appropriate for a country retreat.

New York Public Library

sels shine, you might use this same mix all in one color or white. You might even display them with modern wood and leather pieces and still create a feeling of country warmth.

The only real mistake in creating a country room is to introduce too much grandeur into your rustic environment. Rarely does a retreat featuring gilt and crystal manage to impart a sylvan feeling. More usually, the effect of high-fashion decors transported to rural settings is at best awkward and at worst pompous and artificial.

If you're determined to have opulent surroundings in the country, at least opt for either vernacular or provincial interpretations of high-style furniture. Historically, such pieces were often painted, sometimes with faux wood-grain or marble finishes. Chairs made in New York and elsewhere at the beginning of the nineteenth century decorated with gold leaf and painted landscapes are a good example of vernacular adaptation. Featuring cane, woven wood-strip, or rush seats, which were often cushioned, these chairs imitated the designs of England's Thomas Sheraton (1751–1806). They were called "fancy chairs" and were quite whimsical. Many have a faux bamboo spindle form.

Collections of regional crafts, artwork, and furniture are of course a big part of traditional country rooms. Two-dimensional, stylized like-

nesses painted by itinerant artists who were at work throughout America during the eighteenth and nineteenth centuries automatically suggest a country rather than a city setting. Some of the best—painted by Asahel Lunde Powers (1813–1843) who was active in Vermont, New York, and Connecticut; Ammi Phillips (1788–1865); and Joshua Johnson (circa 1800–1824)—have recently sold for very high prices. Known as primitive art, these portraits of individuals and family groups have the same monumental iconlike presences of Chinese "ancestor portraits." Those depicting children show a particularly endearing quality of innocence or naïveté. Primitive landscapes, such as Edward Hicks' (1780–1849) many versions of the biblical Peaceable Kingdom, are also good choices. It is possible to find excellent reproductions of such works at museum shops and in catalogs, which often make a specialty of selling reproductions from their collections. If you feel squeamish about having a mere copy, by all means commission one of the many folk artists working today to make something special. A view of your town, house, family, or pets will become a treasured heirloom to pass on. Prints, whether engravings, lithographs, woodcuts, or even hand-colored photographs, are perfect decorative accents for country rooms. A tip worth remembering is to always seek prints, books,

LEFT: *Ruffled lace curtains and antique bottles displayed on the window sash are required for those who seek to recapture the solid comfort of the American farm.*

FOLLOWING PAGE: *This magnificent quilt from the collection of Vermont's Shelburne Museum depicts not only a host of images of wild and domestic animals associated with rural American life, but a lion, giraffe, and camel as well.*

123

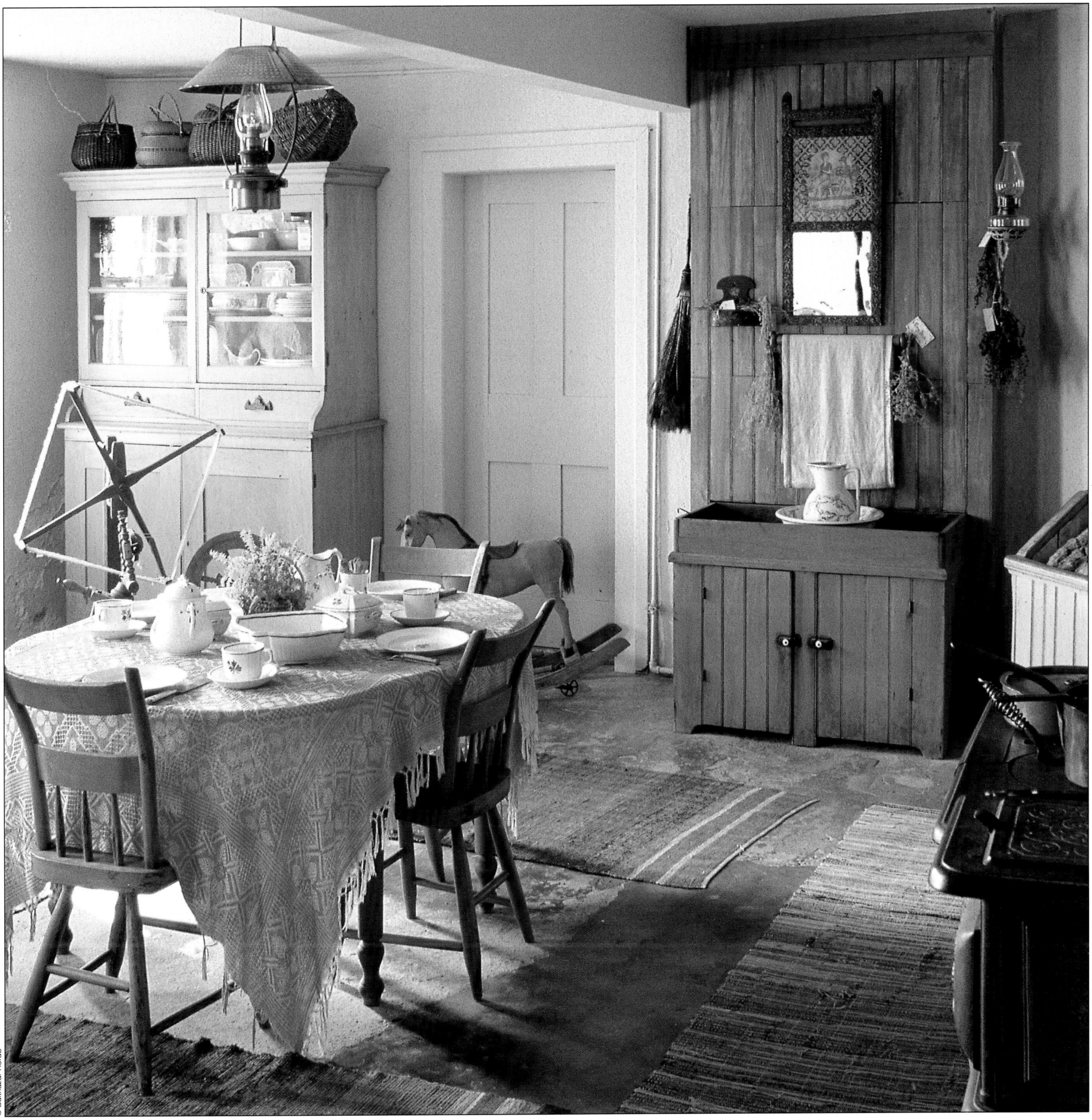

© Balthazar Korab

PRECEDING PAGE: *Even before a wooden floor is laid over the concrete subfloor of this kitchen, a carefully considered collection of rag rugs, old textiles, and rural antiques convinces one that this room must be at least a century old.*

RIGHT: *Spartanly white with hard, shiny enameled and glazed surfaces, this restored turn-of-the-century kitchen has been softened by the introduction of quietly colored paper.*

126

maps, or commemorative plates relating to your region while traveling. Out of town or in another state these images will cost far less than at home. While authentic items like Currier and Ives landscapes are increasingly difficult to find, reproductions look quite presentable when matted and framed. If you have an inexpensive print or even a good photocopy, you can hand-color it and again deceive most people, who will think that it is an exceptional graphic.

Not only are many traditional country crafts, including Amish quilts, stoneware crockery, and various uniquely regional baskets, still made just as they were a hundred years ago, there are also kits

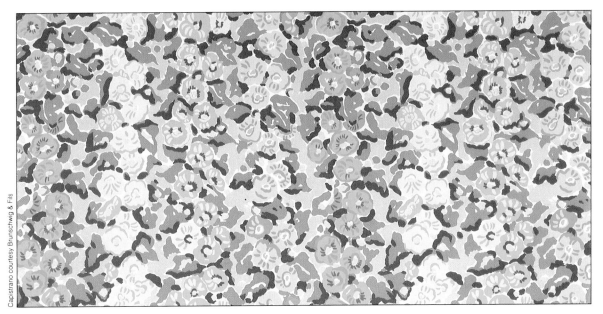

Large cabinets such as hutches, corner cupboards, and vitrines make excellent display cases, but take up lots of room. And remembering Aunt Ethel's grouping of Christmas plates, you may be reluctant to display your collectibles on the wall; don't be, it can be an attractive way to show off your treasures. If you have a collection of plates, for example, consider creating a pattern, or arranging them by color or size. Old shop signs, such as gigantic boots or eyeglasses or even signboards are rare, but more modern signs such as gas-station emblems or neon advertisements possess a similar charm. Displayed on the wall, a distinctive object or a dazzling arrangement can form a strong enough focal point to permit a white background. Just remember that the more exciting and eye-catching your accents are, the more subtle your background can be. Rich color or bold wallpapers will create a more lavish look, and pattern on pattern can be stunning. Care is required, however, because the more complexity you introduce into a space, the more difficult it is to establish control. Like a good meal, a good room needs to find a balance between extravagance and restraint. Finally, be it a mansion or a cottage, it is the ability to combine objects and furniture to produce a relaxed, comfortable, and natural experience that is finally at the heart of the country room.

Flowered prints, as upholstery or wall coverings, add a country flavor.

127

available for making most any item required in a country decor. You can assemble and stencil a wedding chest lined in cedar, embroider rugs and pillows, crochet coverlets and canopies, hook rugs, and throw pottery. Many homeowners take special pride in producing objects for their dwellings, just as their forebears did.

Chapter Six

© Peter Paige

AMERICAN INNOVATIONS

© Nancy Hill

130

PRECEDING PAGE: ***With dining and entertaining areas combined into a single space, opened up to the outdoors by means of a wall of floor-to-ceiling windows, this great room, designed by Lori Margolis, uses two different floor levels as a way to distinguish the two areas. It is as effective as walls without the sense of confinement. Although they look completely up to date, the dining chairs were designed by Frank Lloyd Wright almost ninety years ago.***

ABOVE: ***A combination of living room, kitchen, and dining room, the great room is a targeted solution to the hectic pace of the '90s lifestyle. A situation like this could easily be created by removing a wall to combine a former garage and kitchen or by adding a small wing.***

Like keeping rooms in days of yore, the "great room" of today responds to the needs of families that are active every moment of the day. The great room is usually a combination kitchen, living room, dining room, and family room—a space for eating, entertaining, and living. Although this multiuse room developed out of practical requirements, it has produced airy open expanses that are as beautiful as they are functional. In modern American life, with servants almost unheard of, houses made up of innumerable, specialized divisions have become largely obsolete. If you have a formal dining room with a chandelier and heaps of silver, consider how often you actually use it. And by the way, who keeps all that silver sparkling? Emily Post used to admonish her readers to "have silver that glistens or none at all." (I'm just using silver as an indication of a formal structured lifestyle that's out of step with the way most Americans live now. By all means, don't, for goodness' sake, go and throw out your heirloom tea set! Rather, use it enough that it and your flatware don't need polishing so often.)

If you do use the dining room fairly often, keep it separate; if you don't, consider combining it with your kitchen by replacing the partition with a steel beam and piers. These can be encased in woodwork to match the rest of the room. Other decorative possibilities for these posts abound, depending on the style of room you choose.

A great room can be created in many ways. You may have a garage that adjoins the living room, kitchen, or dining room. You can dramatically increase the value of your house by building a new garage projecting in front of the old one. You might ask, what do you do with the old garage? The answer is, design a great room. To start, insulate the old garage, but be sure to leave the rafters exposed. They can be stained or painted to give the new great room an uplifting architectural quality. Be sure to provide an entrance into the new garage for convenient access.

If the new garage is built directly onto the old one there will be no windows on one wall. However, skylights and clerestory windows (those built way up near the ceiling), along with windows on

One of the reasons that well-to-do Americans fall in love with the Tudor Revival style of the 1920s is the flexibility and grandeur of great halls with spaces for eating, reading, and entertaining, like this one at Stan Hywet Hall built by Goodyear founder Frank Sieberling and designed by Charles Schneider in 1915.

other walls and French doors into the backyard or garden, will more than compensate for any lost light. Because the garage floor is made from concrete, you might consider adding brick or stone flooring, which readily evoke country spaces. Note that it might not otherwise be practical to construct without structural reinforcement. If there's any hint of a problem with dampness, erect a slightly elevated floor with heating ducts underneath. You'll lose some height but it will be well worth it not to suffer discomfort. Many firms supply prefabricated elements like fireplaces and bay windows. Any realtor will tell you that either feature makes a house more desirable. Each will also readily support the country flavor usually imparted by informal great rooms.

Big spaces require amply proportioned objects to keep them from seeming empty. Don't be intimidated—view it as an opportunity. A big space allows you the freedom to own all sorts of things you might have fantasized about but couldn't possibly have fit in your house before the great room. Billiard and ping-pong tables, old jukeboxes with fabulous neon embellishments, and big-screen television sets all become appropriate in a great room. So do quilts used as wall hangings, tapestries, and old signs like the distinctive service station emblems once common along the highways of

Courtesy Stan Hywet Hall, Ohio/photo by H. K. Barnett

131

© Balthazar Korab

Even in a modern apartment building it is possible to have a great room, especially if you acquire raw space in a cooperative or condominium before the apartment has been chopped up into tiny rooms. Because their meals usually take place out-of-doors (except in bad weather), the owners here have been able to combine an art gallery with the infrequently utilized dining area.

America. Chippendale-style highboys, giant rolltop desks, massive Victorian sideboards, and other oversize antiques, which seem overwhelming in regular rooms, have a perfectly proportioned scale for a great room. Cigar store Indians and carousel animals make delightful sculptural accents in lofty rooms. Old wooden porch columns or stoves and other elements salvaged from lost historic buildings can be used to supply interest and definition. If you had six Tuscan columns from an old porch, for instance, you could place them in pairs flanking the fireplace, doors, or windows to give the room more order. Topped with pots of trailing ivy, bright large pottery vases, or Neoclassical statuettes made from plaster, these pillars would give the great room an air of dignity. In order to keep things from getting too stuffy, a pinball machine or video game center could easily be fit in.

Although it requires a little more work to create illumination in a great room, candlelight can be especially enchanting. The relaxed informality typical of most great rooms would suggest something other than a conventional Waterford chandelier; but remember that once you replace electric lights with candles the chandelier takes on an entirely new look. Crystal chandeliers devoid of drops and lighted with candles are especially fashionable in great rooms. Restaurant or theater chandeliers are sometimes required to properly light a great room.

Likewise, tiny plants and flowers that have no impact whatever in great rooms can be replaced by big terra-cotta pots and jars planted with palms, lemon and orange trees, hibiscus, oleander, and gardenias. In summer, these plants can be set into the garden, out on a terrace, or around the pool.

Roman shades and other blinds that can be raised to reveal a view and let in light or lowered to help insulate a room are better in a great room than draw curtains and require less material as well. Shutters, screens, and venetian blinds have similar advantages. Inside or out, a lattice covered with climbing vines forms a wonderful translucent natural curtain. If you aren't interested in keeping the window clear of obstructions, use curtains, but be sure to select a fabric suited to promoting the unpretentious charm that is suggested by the big fireplaces, windows, and wood beams of great rooms.

© Alex McLean

133

L O F T S

It isn't always necessary to alter a space in order to have a great room. Urban lofts in abandoned warehouses and unused factories were rehabilitated by artists in the 1960s all around the nation as living and studio space. Many artists found themselves making great rooms out of the necessity of obtaining inexpensive work and living spaces. They creatively adapted lofts into comfortable homes with great charm. In New York, Boston, Chicago, San Francisco, Los Angeles, and many smaller cities including Cleveland, Seattle, and San Antonio, the one-time artist's loft has become home to young professionals, who came to be known as Yuppies, in the 1980s. The semibohemian spaciousness of lofts, which are very often conveniently located near business centers, appealed to many young urban upwardly mobile professionals. Today, decorated in every sort of style imaginable, lofts appeal to all sorts of people from every walk of life.

Probably no other space is so impressive as an expansive loft in a congested and crowded city. The monochromatic scheme – white, in this case, with turquoise accents – could just as effectively have been some other combination: yellow with cobalt or gray with pink.

134

While a sleek glass and granite contemporary aesthetic is usually associated with an urban loft, this great room, created by designer Hal Bromm, expresses old world charm instead. The sunny yellow walls dispel the gloomy shadows cast by New York's tall buildings.

"They're great for displaying tapestries or gigantic Abstract Expressionist paintings," enthuses one Dallas art dealer. Indeed, the original appeal of lofts, and much of their distinctiveness, comes from the opportunity to display. Accordingly, no matter how people decorate or lay out their lofts, there is usually an attempt to retain something of the openness of the original space. This is, of course, happily compatible with the concept of the great room. Although it might seem that lofts demand an open, loose, informal treatment, other approaches can work. Furniture group-

ings like conversation islands, plants, paintings, and many, many flowers make a great room inviting. Even without architectural elements, symmetrical groups of furniture arranged against the walls almost as if they were columns, can lend the great room an architectural sense. Even when walls are left white, which can be rather bleak, using strong colors, such as red or even turquoise for upholstery, repeated often in the carpets and accessories, will will offset the blank walls. With bright sunlight, the effect is crisp and clean, but not at all messy or informal.

135

BEACH STYLE

As with other regional buildings, American beach houses come in every size and shape. Generally, though, they share big windows, sheltering porches, and balconies, allowing for maximum enjoyment of the outdoors. The combination of waves, scented breezes, and shimmering sun has attracted beach fanciers for centuries. Shore communities include rustic Adirondack camps, enclaves along placid Lake Tahoe, and resort towns adjacent to the magnificent freshwater inland seas, modestly called the Great Lakes. The sea coasts of both the Eastern and Western United States resonate most clearly of summer pleasures at the shore, however. On the Atlantic coast, from Seal Harbor to the Barrier Islands of Georgia and South Carolina, "cottages," as modest as a one-room Nantucket shack or as elegant as a shingled Queen Anne–style mansion in the Hamptons, exemplify the Eastern version of beach style. The Pacific Ocean has also given rise to distinctive seashore shelter. At San Simeon or Monterey in California, white frame

The very idea of beach style is exemplified by this outdoor dining spot with tranquil water views framed by palm trees.

This porch, overlooking a neighboring house with a fanciful observation tower designed by architect Deborah Berke, brings back the best qualities of American resort architecture, which has enjoyed a renaissance in seaside Florida.

136

This unstuffy house design is an answer for Americans yearning for a return to fun in architecture after decades of modernism.

houses of one or two stories look out over tranquil beaches of smooth pebbles adorned with natural sculptures of driftwood carved by the sea. Recalling the state's strong Spanish heritage, Californian beachfront haciendas of stucco with tile roofs are also frequently found at Montecito and at San Luis Obispo. As one might expect, many West Coast regional beach houses have been built in a spare, stylized manner, betraying the dramatic influence of Hollywood. Huge picture windows, some of which slide into the wall or sink into the floor, transform the houses into little more than an open porch beside the surf.

Florida and the Texas Gulf coast also have unique regional architecture that expresses and celebrates beach living. The 1920s Mediterranean-style homes, half Spanish, half Italian, popularized at Miami, Palm Beach, and Coral Gables, Florida, by architect-developer and self-proclaimed genius Addison Mizner, are still bewitchingly evocative of romance. In the same way, the exuberant Victorian extravaganzas found at Galveston, Texas, have a fairy-tale quality about them.

In the past, regional beach style has been preserved in new houses by exactly replicating old

examples, but this tendency is giving way to a new sensibility. Today, the best beach houses demonstrate subtle references to a local building tradition or material, but they are nevertheless new in attitude and unmistakably all-American in design. It is possible to identify two dominant types of beach house: the Hamptons cottage of the East Coast and the Malibu beach house of the Western seashore.

Just as coastlines, east and west, are at once different and similar, so might beach houses east and west seem very much alike to those unfamiliar with them. For their owners, though, the slight adjustments those structures have made to local climate and custom make all the difference. For instance, even though houses found at Bridgehampton, Long Island, and at Pebble Beach, California, have evolved for a common purpose of enjoying life at the beach close to a big city, houses at both places are as distinct as the dunes versus cliffs and white quartz versus honey-colored sands of their beaches—at least, that is, to natives. For many other people, though, the houses might not seem to differ at all other than in the plant material found in their gardens. What is it that sets apart the regional rooms of the modern beach house?

138

ABOVE LEFT: *Imparting tradition and romance to a decor depends not so much on copying old regional rooms as in distilling their essence, as in this room by architect Ben Moore. Wicker, floral chintz, and many windows will always be at home in the country.*

ABOVE RIGHT: *Trompe l'oeil wall paintings in this double height porch (by architects Bartos and Rhodes, design by McMillen, Inc.) provide just the right amount of visual interest.*

OPPOSITE PAGE: *Hung with old weathervanes with antique forks propped against the post and sheets of glass replacing original rough red siding, this barn makes a magically All-American setting for the swimming pool.*

The typical summer cottage of the 1890s along the Eastern seashore was a rambling structure with many gables, wraparound porches, and bedrooms for everyone from servants to in-laws to fourth cousins once removed. Once, those dinosaurs were found in hospitable groupings from Kennebunkport, Maine to Palm Beach, Florida. Today, however, social and private lives are not quite so well organized. Modern East Coast beach houses no longer resemble the small private hotels that their predecessors emulated. Often, a beach house is meant to function as a personal refuge from the stress of city life. Indeed, in order to assure maximum privacy, many modern-day beach cottages are just that: tiny, open structures, with no more than a couple of bedrooms at most adjoining a large multipurpose living, cooking, and eating space, known as a great room. The indispensable screened porch is where you can usually find everyone. Occasional guests can be put up on the big overstuffed sofa covered in a cheerful floral chintz, usually found on

the porch in addition to white, green, or natural wicker furniture.

The big great rooms found in Hamptons beach houses were inspired by old barns, which were common until about thirty years ago, when potato farms still surrounded the big estates along the shore. Most of the turn-of-the-century estates and the older farms alike have been broken up into sites for building weekend cottages and smaller summer houses. After World War II, converting venerable farm buildings into houses became a major local business. Enormous expanses of windows were added to the sturdy rough oaken framework, and instant gardens were created below old orchards. Former hen houses made great bathhouses for the swimming pool.

The spaciousness of the Hamptons' barn houses and the great rooms that are their modern heirs at the beach often incorporate other elements of the region's architectural history. A local tradition of big rambling Colonial Revival – or Queen

Using a single wall color throughout an interior adds to the spacious sense of this beach house living room, designed by Suzanne Kelly, which takes its color from the quilt borders. This wall color treatment also aids in forming a progressive relationship from one room into the next.

140

Anne–style residences is recalled by the introduction of large round or arched Palladian windows in those rooms. Wicker, rattan, and wire porch and terrace furniture from the Gilded Era of the early 1900s is also finding its way into great rooms at the beach. Because they are often two-and-a-half stories high, these rooms stay cool in summer. Ceiling fans have become a popular means of blowing the warm air down or drawing it up, depending on the season. Interior shutters are also favored because they don't obscure any of the enchanting water views when open and provide ventilated privacy when closed.

Although it can be a difficult color to work with, white is the color most frequently chosen in beach houses on the East Coast as opposed to the strong pastels generally found out West. The most painless means of using white successfully with almost no other color in the room is to use old barn beams (or new ones) bleached or painted white.

Painted bare wooden floors are particularly practical at the beach, as are floors of brick, stone, or tile. Straw and sisal mats make perfect floor coverings—they are both attractive and easy to work with. Painted furniture or dark wooden antiques with light-colored leather upholstery or washable plain or printed cotton or linen slipcovers are often found at Hamptons beach houses. Outside, privet hedges that frame views, driveways, gardens, and pools impart privacy and a unique style to the region. Mock orange, spirea, lilac, daisy, foxglove, delphinium, zinnia, and above all, old-fashioned scented roses are staples found in area gardens. Their blooms fill yellowware, crocks, aluminum florist cans, blue and white china, and a host of other vases appropriate for the ubiquitous fresh bouquets that are essential to beach houses.

Whereas white, sometimes in combination with other colors, is typical in the Hamptons, West Coast beach houses more often employ the joyous

Out West, the sun at the beach is stronger than on the East Coast so that it's possible to indulge a taste for luscious colors like the blue and violet displayed in these rooms. The focal Chippendale Rococo mirror forms an appealing tension with the gently rolled chair backs and streamlined table.

colors of the local scene. Just as natural light in America is stronger than the mist-filtered light of England, and muted colors that seem attractive in the British Isles often look washed out in the United States, so too the soft palette of East Coast rooms seems anemic in California. Many Californians favor clear pastels such as lavender, lemon yellow, lime green, and hot pink—all of these ice-cream colors grace Malibu dwellings. Often built on pilings above the high tide or flood level, West Coast beach houses enjoy a more even and tranquil climate. As a result, houses there have an even greater glass-to-solid-wall ratio than on the Atlantic coast.

West Coast beach houses are also often lower in height than their Eastern counterparts. Great rooms, although they tend to be somewhat larger, are often less lofty as a result. On the other hand, because so many skilled craftspeople live in the area, architectural tours de force such as domed or barrel-vaulted ceilings are not uncommon.

Evocative of Spanish Colonial design, rooms sheltered by such unusual ceilings make perfect settings for the handmade furniture designed by such West Coast artisans as designer-decorator Rose Tarlow. High-backed armchairs with spiral or saber-shaped legs, ladder-back side chairs with tasseled cushions, or elaborately carved and painted chests give these rooms polish without pomposity. The white linen and cotton chintz slipcovers often seen in the East are also popular in the West. However, the slate floors often used in the East are passed over on the West Coast in favor of traditional tile, or the more glamorous, but still easy-to-clean, marble.

Palms, hibiscus, jasmine, and other exotic plants usually surround the swimming pool (people on both coasts have come to regard pools as essential—in addition to the ocean) and lend a semi-tropical Paradise-like ambience eagerly cultivated by Californians.

SOURCES

Arizona

Arizona Design Center
3600 East University Dr
Phoenix, AZ 85034
602/232-0032

California

South Coast Design Center
at Stonemill
2915 Redhill Ave
Costa Mesa, CA 92626
714/979-8200

Design Center South
23811 Aliso Creed Rd
Laguna Niguel, CA 92677
714/643-2929

Los Angeles Home
Furnishings Mart
1933 S Broadway
Los Angeles, CA 90007
213/749-7911

Pacific Design Center
8687 Melrose Ave
Los Angeles (W Hollywood),
CA 90069
213/657-0800

Atrium Design Center
69–930 Hwy 111
Rancho Mirage, CA 92270
619/321-5354

Canyon Creek Design Center
of San Diego, Inc.
4041–4330 Morena Blvd
San Diego, CA 92117
619/483-1741

San Diego Design Center
6455 Lusk Blvd
San Diego, CA 92121
619/452-SDDC

200 Kansas
200 Kansas St
San Francisco, CA 94103
415/522-2290

Galleria Design Center
101 Henry Adams St
San Francisco, CA 94103
415/846-1500

Colorado

Design Center at the Ice House
1801 Wynkoop St
Denver, CO 80202
303/298-9191

Denver Design Center
595 S Broadway
Denver, CO 80209-4001
303/733-2455

Denver Merchandise Mart
451 East 58 Ave
Denver, CO 80216
303/292-MART

District of Columbia

Washington Design Center
300 D St SW
Washington, DC 20024
202/554-5053

Florida

Design Center of the Americas
1855 Griffin Rd
Dania, FL 33004
305/920-7997

Miami International Design
Center 1
4100 Northeast Second Ave
Miami, FL 33137
305/573-8224

Georgia

Atlanta Decorative Arts Center
351 Peachtree Hills Ave NE
Atlanta, GA 30305
404/231-1720

Atlanta Merchandise Mart
240 Peachtree St NW
Atlanta, GA 30043
404/220-2121

Illinois

Merchandise Mart
Merchandise Mart Center
Chicago, IL 60654
312/527-4141

Massachusetts

Boston Design Center
One Design Center Place
Boston, MA 02210
617/388-5062

Michigan

Michigan Design Center
1700 Stutz Dr
Troy, MI 48084
313/649-4772

Minnesota

International Market Square
275 Market St
Minneapolis, MN 55405
612/338-6250

Missouri

Saint Louis Design Center
917 Locust
St. Louis, MO 63101
314/621-6446

North Carolina

Hamilton Wrenn Community
of Showrooms
200 North Hamilton St
High Point, NC 27260
919/884-0075

International Home
Furnishings Center
210 East Commerce St
High Point, NC 27261
919/889-6144

Market Square
305 W High St
High Point, NC 27260
919/889-4464

Nevada

Centerpoint Park
4040 South Industrial
Las Vegas, NV 89103
702/369-0707

New York

Architects & Designers
Building
A & D Building
150 East 58 St/964 Third Ave
New York, NY 10155
212/644-6555

Decoration & Design Building
979 Third Ave
New York, NY 10022
212/759-2964

Decorative Arts Center
305 East 63 St
New York, NY 10021
212/838-7736

Decorator's Center Building
315 East 62 St
New York, NY 10021
212/682-4737

Fine Arts Building
232 East 59 St
New York, NY 10022
212/759-6935

International Design Center,
New York Center Two
30–20 Thomson Ave
Long Island City, NY 11101
718/937-7474

International Showcase
225 Fifth Ave
New York, NY 10010
212/685-6377

Manhattan Art &
Antique Center
1050 Second Ave
New York, NY 10022
212/355-4400

Marketcenter
230 Fifth Ave
New York, NY 10001
212/532-4555

New York Design Center
200 Lexington Ave
New York, NY 10016
212/679-9500

Place Des Antiquaires
125 East 57 St
New York, NY 10022
212/758-2709

Ohio

Ohio Design Center
23533 Mercantile Rd
Beachwood, OH 44122
216/621-7619

Pendleton Square Design Center
1118 Pendleton St
Cincinnati, OH 45210
513/621-7619

St. Paul's Mart
1117 Pendleton St
Cincinnati, OH 45210
513/579-1922

Oregon

Design Center at
Montgomery Park
2701 Northwest Vaughn St
Portland, OR 97210
503/228-7275

Pennsylvania

Marketplace Design Center
2400 Market St
Philadelphia, PA 19103
215/561-5000

Texas

Dallas Decorative Center
Dallas, TX 75207
214/744-4212

Dallas Design Center
1025 North Stemmons Frwy
Dallas, TX 75207
214/747-2411

Dallas Home Furnishings Mart
2000 N. Stemmons Frwy
Dallas, TX 75201
214/655-6134

Dallas Market Center
2100 Stemmons Frwy
Dallas, TX 75207
214/655-6100

Dallas World Trade Center
2050 Stemmons Frwy
Dallas, TX 75207
214/655-6100

Design District & Contract
Design Center
1400 Turtle Creek Blvd
Dallas, TX 75207
214/744-4212

Oak Lawn Plaza
1444 Oaklawn Ave
Dallas, TX 75207
214/689-4222

Decorative Center of Houston
5120 Woodway Dr
Houston, TX 77056
713/961-9292

Innova
20 Greenway Plaza
Houston, TX 77046
800/237-0617

Interior Resource Center of
Houston
7026 Old Katy Rd
Houston, TX 77024
713/861-2114

Utah

Showplace Square
522 South 400 W
Salt Lake City, UT 84101
801/355-0519

Washington

6100 Building
6100 Fourth Ave S
Seattle, WA 98108
206/767-6800

Lenora Square
1000 Lenora St
Seattle, WA 98121
206/621-7500

Design Center Northwest
5701 Sixth Ave S
Seattle, WA 98108
206/762-1200

FURTHER READING | INDEX

Baldwin, Billy. *Billy Baldwin Decorates* Holt, Rinehart & Winston: 1972.

Bedford, Steven. *The Long Island Country House 1870–1930* Perpetua Press: 1988.

Bishop, Robert. *The American Chair* Bonanza Books: 1983.

Boutells, Sara Holmor. *Julia Morgan Architect* Abbeville Press: 1988.

Bunting, Bainbridge. *The Houses of Boston's Backbay* Belkamp Press: 1967.

Compon, Richard. *Ohio An Architectural Portrait* West Summit Press: 1973.

Comstock, Helen. *100 Most Beautiful Rooms in America* Bonanza Books: 1958.

DeNevi, Donald and Thomas Moulin. *Gabris Moulins Peninsula* Windgate Press: 1985.

Emerling, Mary. *American Country* Clarkson Potter: 1988.

Eston, John. *Manhattan Style* Little, Brown & Co.: 1990.

Ferree, Bart. *American Estates And Gardens* Munn & Co.: 1904.

Harris, Bill. *Grand Homes of the Midwest* Crescent Books: 1990.

Irvine, Chippy. *The Town House* Bantam: 1989.

Johnson, Shirley. *Palm Beach Houses* Rizzoli: 1991.

Lowe, David. *Chicago Interiors* Contemporary Books: 1979.

Micheller, Robert William. *Classic Savanna* Gold Coast: 1987.

Mitchell, Henry. *Washington Houses of the Capital* Viking Press: 1982.

O'Neal, William B. and Christopher Weeks. *The Work of William Lawrence Bottomley in Richmond* University Press of Virginia: 1985.

Patterson, Agusta Owens. *American Homes Today* The MacMillan Co.: 1924.

Schuler, Stanley. *New England Homes* Schiffer Publishing Ltd.: 1984.

Sirkis, Nancy. *Newport Pleasures and Palaces* Viking Press: 1963.

Stern, Robert. *Pride of Place* Houghton Mifflin Co.: 1986.

Tweed, Katherine. *The Finest Rooms by America's Great Decorators* Viking Press: 1964.

Williams, Henry L. with Ottalick Williams. *America's Small Houses* Bonanza Books: 1963.

Wright, Richardson. *House and Garden's Complete Guide to Interior Decoration* Simon and Schuster: 1942.

143